A CUP OF COMFORT® *for a* Better World

Stories that celebrate those who give, care, and volunteer

Edited by
Colleen Sell

Avon, Massachusetts

With gratitude to Copthorne MacDonald, whose erudite book Matters of Consequence, *which I had the good fortune to edit, illuminates the path toward a better tomorrow and inspired me to do my part today.*

Published by
Adams Media, a division of F+W Media, Inc.
57 Littlefield Street, Avon, MA 02322 U.S.A.
www.adamsmedia.com and *www.cupofcomfort.com*

ISBN 10: 1-4405-0210-2
ISBN 13: 978-1-4405-0210-1

Printed in the United States of America.

10 9 8 7 6 5 4 3 2 1

Library of Congress Cataloging-in-Publication Data
is available from the publisher.

This book is available at quantity discounts for bulk purchases.
For information, please call 1-800-289-0963.

Contents

You Bought Me Sleep • Shelley Seale 1

As You Are Able • Joan Watt 11

I Always Have Time for You • Wm. Scott Hubbartt 16

Angels Afoot • Lisa Ricard Claro 21

The Rubber Chicken Cure • Michele Ivy Davis 26

If We Eat Less, They Can Eat More

    • Connie Rosser Riddle 31

The Sweetest Gift • Betsy McPhee 40

Where Magic Lives • Jan Philpot 45

All It Takes Is an Open Heart • Grace Tierney 51

Of Worth and Grace • Lyndell King 57

Beyond the Classroom • Eloise Elaine Schneider 63

Fixing a Faucet while Mending a Soul

    • Marlena Thompson 68

Small Change Today, Philanthropy Tomorrow

    • Sue Dallman-Carrizales 73

A Legacy to Carry On • Irene Martin 80

Making a Dent • Susan Sarver 88

The Benevolence of Mindfulness
    • Tanya Ward Goodman 95

Generosity Knows No Stranger • Sybilla A. Cook 100

The Face Beneath the Hood • Beth Levine 105

Trash Talk • Stefanie Wass 108

The Power of Pebbles • Cristina Trapani-Scott 114

Child by Child • Linda Stork 119

Heroes on Harleys • Christina Suzann Nelson 126

Quit Talkin' and Start Doin'
    • Betty Johnson Dalrymple 132

The Coat off Her Back • Deborah Royal 140

An Oasis of Hope in a Harrowing World
    • Trudy Chun 145

The Gratitude Effect • Sharon Elwell 152

A Lift Up—Not a Handout
    • Linda Hudson Hoagland 157

Forgiving the Unforgivable • Mary Long 165

A Better World for $50 or Less • Ann Vitale 170

In Lila's Shoes • Carol Tyx 175

Touching Souls • Eleanor Roth 184

Guardian Angels • Lea Ellen Yarmill Reburn 190

A Little Can Be a Lot • Elizabeth Sharpe 196

One Less to Count Up • John Forrest 202

Stepping Out of My Comfort Zone • Ava Pennington . . .211

Upon a Midnight Clear • Linda S. Clare 216

Frugality: It's Not Just about Penny-Pinching Anymore

    • Beverly Golberg. 223

No Prescription Needed • Sue Fagalde Lick 231

The Real Santa Claus • Alaina Smith 236

Bangles, Bubbles, and Blue-Collar Kindness

    • J. K. Fleming 243

Gifts of Sustenance and Sanctuary • Mirish Kiszner 251

Jumping In • Suzanne Baginskie. 259

More Blessed to Give • Anne McCrady 267

His Neighbor's Keeper • Fran Roberts. 275

Bless the Beasts and the Teenyboppers

    • Marcia Rudoff 281

Circle of Compassion • Laura Bradford. 288

Not Interested • Eloise Elaine Schneider 295

A Village Built with Ink and Dreams

    • Samantha Ducloux Waltz 299

To Do Small Things with Great Love

    • Christy Caballero 308

Contributors. 317

About the Editor 326

Acknowledgments

I was raised by two people who are so conscientious, so generous, so compassionate, and so honorable that, as a kid, I dubbed them Mr. and Mrs. Dudley Do-Right. So I must first thank my parents for teaching me, through their example, the importance of doing good.

As always, I am thankful to the terrific team at Adams Media for their good judgment in publishing a book about altruism in action and for all their professional and personal support—especially Meredith O'Hayre, the captain of the *Cup of Comfort*® ship, and Paula Munier, its creator.

I am most grateful to the writers whose inspiring stories grace these pages . . . and to you, dear readers, for your interest in reading about the good hearts and good works of others.

Introduction

". . . *anybody can serve. You don't have to have a college degree to serve. You don't have to make your subject
and verb agree to serve. You only need a heart full of
grace. A soul generated by love."*
— *Dr. Martin Luther King, Jr.*

I've always found it interesting that most religions
and spiritual belief systems implore us to "love one
another," to love not only our family and friends but
also our neighbors. Some ask us to love strangers,
even our enemies. And some cast the love net even
farther—to encompass all sentient beings, the Earth
itself, and the vast universe beyond our telescopes
and our imaginations. Many of these faiths (for lack
of a better, all-encompassing term) also call upon
us to nurture and protect children and nature, to

care for those who cannot care for themselves, and to show compassion for "the least among" us—the sick, the poor, the lost, the fallen, the weary. It is a tall order. It is also, in my humble opinion, the key to making the world a better place.

Love *alone* is not the answer. Love is not *all* we need. Solving the world's problems and righting the world's wrongs also takes understanding, compassion, resources, and courage. But love lights the fire of "loving-kindness" (the desire to "do good") in our bellies and fuses together all of those other components into a powerful force for good. For, when we truly love someone or something, we can't help but care. We strive to understand. We find the strength and the resources to help, to comfort, to heal, to give. We endeavor *not* to harm or hinder. And we do not, cannot, just look away or walk away; our heart and our conscience simply will not allow it.

While love is charity's catalyst, it seems that fear, greed, and ignorance are its inhibitors. It has been said that "the confused mind says no." As it turns out, so does fearful or glutinous thinking. When someone doesn't recognize or understand someone else's problem (or a problem they think is someone else's but, in reality, also adversely affects them), they are less likely to care about and do something about it. Same goes when someone is afraid that there is not enough of whatever it is—food, money, medicine, good will—to go around, that giving to others might deprive or somehow jeopardize them or theirs. And the greedy, well, if they cared about others, if they loved others as they love themselves, they would be giving rather than gobbling everything up with little or no thought to the world around them.

So it is up to the rest of us to do our parts, individually and collectively, to make a positive difference in the world—or in the life of a single other person or being—and to encourage others to do the same. One way to inspire kindness and charity is to share personal stories about random acts of kindness and about people who are helping to make the world a better place. And who knows? Maybe such stories will open the minds and hearts of some of those folks who "say no" to giving out of fear, ignorance, or greed. I hope so.

And I hope the stories in *A Cup of Comfort® for a Better World* warm your heart and light the fire of loving-kindness in your belly.

—*Colleen Sell*

You Bought Me Sleep

The idea of volunteering in another country has long been considered the province of students and recent graduates; images of intrepid, twenty-year-old Peace Corps workers in a remote Sierra Leone village might spring to mind. Today, however, the idea has reached far beyond and become an accessible and highly popular pursuit among travelers of all ages and backgrounds. Volunteer travel has grown so popular that a term has even been coined for it: "voluntourism." Foreign destinations are luring American citizens who want to sightsee while simultaneously engaging in community service. Companies and websites specializing in voluntourism have sprung up by the hundreds, and volunteer vacations can be found in all parts of the world, doing all kinds of activities—from digging wells for clean water in South America, to protecting the elephant population in South Africa, to working with children living in orphanages.

It was this last type of volunteer vacation that hooked me. In 2004, I became involved with a non-profit based in Austin, Texas, called The Miracle Foundation, which manages orphanages in India and recruits sponsors and donors to support the children living there. I began volunteering for the foundation and sponsored a ten-year-old boy named Santosh, living in the state of Orissa in northeastern India. Caroline Boudreaux, founder of the organization, soon invited me to accompany her and a group of other volunteers to Orissa. So it was that in March 2005, I found myself in India for the first time, on a ten-day volunteer trip that I was to make, it turned out, many more times over the years since.

The village is remote, and it took forty-eight hours of exhausting travel to reach the ashram where the children live. By the time we arrived, all ten volunteers in the group were suffering from sleep deprivation and culture shock: The overwhelming throngs of people. The new sights, smells, and sounds that awakened all the senses at once. The frantic streets filled with bicycles, rickshaws, cars, and cows, with the constant beep-beep of horns blaring above it all. And, especially, the relentless poverty that does not let you rest.

Caroline had briefed us well on both India and on what to expect during our week at the orphanage. But nothing could have prepared me for what I felt when we entered those gates. Dozens of children were lined around the drive in a semi-circle, waving and chanting "welcome" over and over. I climbed out and they swarmed all over me, reaching for my hands and touching my feet in blessing. I was inundated, lost in the sea of small bodies—smiling, barefoot children who asked nothing from me other than simply being there.

As I would soon learn, in India these "invisible" children are everywhere; they fill the streets, the railway stations, the villages. Thirty thousand Indian babies are born HIV-positive each year; many become orphans when their mothers succumb to AIDS. Indeed, millions of Indian children are orphaned by AIDS, malaria, or simple infections. Some are orphaned due to nothing more than poverty; their parents cannot afford to feed them. Orphanages and other institutional homes are overflowing, leaving many kids to live alone on the streets, parentless and homeless. Amidst the growing prosperity of India, there is an entire generation of children growing up without parents—more than 25 million in all. A shocking number of them are trafficked as indentured laborers or prostitutes. Others are forced into child labor or prostitution by their own parents to pay off debts or feed the family.

But there in Choudwar, a small town about 100 miles south of Calcutta, one man named Damodar Sahoo has dedicated his life to providing a home and family for some of these children. Before The Miracle Foundation, he constantly lacked enough food, clothing, and supplies to adequately provide for those he had taken in—children who had nowhere else to turn.

On my first trip to India, Mr. Sahoo, known to everyone simply as "Papa," greeted the volunteers heartily, chewing the betel nut that turned his teeth red. While he gave us a tour of the compound, the children trailed us, rushing past each other to claim a volunteer's hand. They were everywhere, always underfoot, craving our attention. As I walked along, four or five clung to each arm; when I sat down, they filled my lap, their slight frames making barely an imprint against my clothing.

I spent the following days just being with the kids, befriending them, playing with them. Our days at the ashram were filled with games, reading, dancing, and laughing. There were puzzles, English flash cards, hopscotch, Frisbee, and the hokey-pokey, which the children wanted to do over and over once it was taught to them. I began to discover their individual personalities, interests, and dreams.

Over that week, I watched the shy ones come out of their shells and their self-confidence blossom. As it did, their best behavior fell away and they became normal kids, not always sweet and perfect, often mischievous as well. When the children thought I wasn't looking, they would shove each other out of the way or bestow thunks on one another's heads in annoyance. They used the language barrier to their advantage, pretending at times not to understand when the adult volunteers said it was time to put a game away, reminding me of my daughter when she was young and seemingly deaf to the word "no."

We began to make friends, and I discovered that the children were just as curious about us and our lives as we were about them. The kids spoke varying levels of English, largely dependent on how many years they had been living in the ashram and attending school. Some had a large vocabulary and good conversational skills; others spoke little more than a few words of English. I found it was surprisingly easy, however, to communicate without sharing even a word of common language. In many ways they were just like other children I've known, children with homes and families of their own—except for their neediness, their raw hunger for affection, love, belonging.

In the midst of the games, laughter, and silliness that we engaged in all day long, I would sometimes forget that they were orphans. When that reality came crashing back, it never failed to hit me with the same painful, breathless intensity it had the first time . . . especially when it intruded unexpectedly, as happened one afternoon.

Caroline and Papa had arranged an ice cream party. Two tables were pulled into the courtyard as the frozen cartons were delivered. The kids lined up eagerly, from youngest to oldest, to be handed their paper cups of ice cream as we scooped it out in a battle of time against the sun blazing overhead. As we served the icy treats and listened to the kids slurping away, I noticed that Santosh, the boy I sponsored, was nowhere to be seen. I asked some of the other boys about him, and they pointed toward the top of the stairs. I went up and found him sitting alone, seeming sad and listless. He wasn't interested in the ice cream.

A house mother named Madhu passed, and I asked her to help me find out what was wrong; I was afraid Santosh was hurt or sick. Madhu took him into the boy's dorm and talked to him for several minutes.

"He misses his mother," she said simply when she came back out.

I sat with Santosh on the edge of the concrete walkway outside his dorm room. Draping my arm around his shoulders, I squeezed reassuringly and held him against my side. I knew that his mother had died when he was so young he couldn't possibly remember her, not really; but to mourn the idea of a mother, that huge absence in his life like a great gaping hole, was another thing completely. We sat together, not speaking, while in the courtyard in front of us the other children slurped up their ice cream.

I felt his loss deep in my heart, and I realized that, although the kids loved us being there, it sometimes only made them miss their own parents. To be sure, they benefited greatly from the attention of all these nurturing surrogate parent figures—Papa, Caroline, the house mothers, the volunteers. But amidst all the caring, love, and joy that filled the ashram, it was sometimes easy to miss the sadness that lingered in the children's tender souls. I was reminded anew that they all carried grief and damage inside them, often hidden or temporarily forgotten but never erased entirely.

Far from the tourist's India of the Taj Mahal and yoga retreats, a journey into an Indian orphanage is a difficult one—hard on the body, hard on the heart. Still, these children living under Papa's care are the lucky ones. In homes like The Miracle Foundation where children are well taken care of, it's far too easy to forget how many street kids are outside those gates—the children sleeping under plastic roofs beside a sewage-filled canal. In the best institutional facilities for orphans, there is love and community and needs are met on the most basic sustenance levels. There never seems to be enough food, never enough medical care, and never enough room. For every child fortunate enough to live in an orphanage or a home like The Miracle Foundation, there are a thousand more that they do not have the room or resources to take in. A thousand more orphans who have nowhere else to turn but to homes run under vastly inferior, sometimes horrific, conditions. A thousand more kids living on the streets, begging at train stations, working twelve hours a day for pennies or selling their bodies to survive. A thousand more children who have been abandoned and whose childhoods have been discarded.

The beautiful kids at Papa's home no longer had their own parents, yet they were still joyful and filled with hope. Their optimism and resilience amazed me time and again. Their ability to overcome crippling challenges inspired me. Their generous spirits humbled me. They served us before eating themselves and offered us seconds of their precious food.

They rushed to bring water, pull up a chair for us, take our shoes off and put them back on, carry our bags—anything and everything. Even in the most deprived circumstances, they were still just kids. They laughed and played, though perhaps less frequently and lightheartedly than more privileged children. They developed strong bonds and relationships with their surrogate parents and with one another, creating family where none existed. Most of all, they had an enormous amount of love to share.

After spending a week at the ashram—having borne witness to the sorrow and scars the past had carved into the children's hearts, having discovered the stories behind the names, having come to know and love the personalities behind the faces—I simply could not go on with my life afterward as if they did not exist. And so I embarked on a three-year journey to write a book, *The Weight of Silence*, to give these children voices and tell their stories. I also continued to return to The Miracle Foundation homes every year to volunteer.

From that first visit, it has been clear to me that Papa and Caroline are doing something special, something more than can be seen with the eyes. Papa, the heart of the ashram, is an almost tangible presence of love. He gave up a far easier life and job as a government official to dedicate himself to these orphans, for which he is paid a small allowance as the director. It is not an easy existence. He doesn't regard himself as remarkable or noble, however, and appears detached from all things material.

"I am a simple beggar," he said, earnestly. "I need nothing, except for these children, my family."

Caroline told me that as she raised money for the orphanage to build a new wing, bunk beds, and bathrooms for the children, she had repeatedly asked Papa to let The Miracle Foundation make some improvements to his small quarters.

"Let me do something for you," she implored Papa.

"No, no. I need nothing," he answered.

"Let me buy you something," Caroline persisted.

But Papa only shook his head, gesturing toward the new dormitories, the children in their uniforms going to school. "You have already bought me the most important thing," he said. "You bought me sleep."

—Shelley Seale

A version of this story appears in the author's book The Weight of Silence: India's Invisible Children, Dog's Eye View Media, June 2009.

As You Are Able

You may have seen her. She's the little gray-haired lady driving down the road talking to herself. You've probably chuckled as you craned your neck to see if someone was sitting beside her; then you probably laughed as her heavy foot shot her car forward as the light turned green. That's my sister, Norma. She's on a mission, and she is talking to someone—God. She prays every mile she travels.

If you open her car door, it may smell of Indiana Fried Chicken. She stops frequently to pick up a few drumsticks to take to the people on her list to visit that day. There is always a piece of homemade lemon pie or caramel iced cake, too, to go with the chicken.

Family members laugh and call her the "happy bag lady," because she always has several in each hand when she arrives at her destination. In an effort to "go green," some of the local stores are selling cloth bags for ninety-nine cents, and we think Norma has surely purchased every one in town. As she goes about her day, she is apt to say to whomever she visits, "I love these bags, I'll leave you one." The bags are easier for her to carry than paper and plastic bags, and she likes to think she is doing her part for the environment.

Her destination might be the health care center, as it is on this particular day. Once inside, she greets the ladies in the entrance hall with, "How are you today?" and gently pats their hands, knowing the importance of a warm touch. She never fails to compliment each of them on what they're wearing. They often return her compliment, today admiring her dressy black jacket.

The nurses, too, wave to Norma as she heads down the hall to our brother Bob's room. The oldest of four siblings, Bob has cared for us through the years; now it's our turn to care for him. She fills his top drawer with all sorts of candy, cookies, and chips, and then stuffs his refrigerator with cheese sticks, soft drinks, puddings, and watermelon.

Bob is just as giving, and he shares what Norma brings to him with others who sit in the hallway waiting and hoping for a visit from someone. She even takes him a huge bag of Dum Dum suckers, which he hands out to the little ones who come with their parents to visit family members. One of the nurses made him a pouch that drapes over the arm of his wheelchair. He stuffs it with suckers. Not only does he delight the children with these treats, he also shares them with his bingo-playing friends.

Today, Norma follows Bob's motorized chair into the dining room, where three attractive ladies are chatting with each other at a dining room table. Bob reaches out and touches one of them. She smiles nicely, nodding her head toward him as she says, "Why, hello Bob." He turns to his sister and introduces the ladies as his bingo partners. Norma listens and then makes a note of their names in a little book she carries in her oversized purse.

Later that day, she shows me the names and explains why she jotted them down. "Calling older people by their given name makes them feel special."

Having noticed another name on the page she held out to me, I ask, "Who is Mason?"

"Well," she begins, "today we were sitting in the front lobby when this young boy hopped out of a car and came running in. He looked to be about ten years old. I was surprised when he ran right up to Bob and hugged him. He pulled a chair up close, sat down, put his hand over Bob's hand, and began talking to him as if he knew him."

Meanwhile, the car and driver that had brought Mason to the center waited in the front of the building. Bob and the young boy laughed and talked to one another, sharing stories. Finally, the boy told Bob he had to go because his dad had left a family reunion to bring him for a visit. They hugged, and Mason kissed Bob on the cheek before waving his hand over his head as he ran to the door.

Bob said to Norma, "What could be more devastating to a ten-year-old boy than losing his best friend, his grandpa?" Then he talked of how most kids spend hours with their grandparents.

Norma says she thought Bob drifted away for a minute as he remembered that our grandmother had died at age fifty-five.

"Age isn't a factor with a child," Bob added. "They don't see the thinning hair, the wrinkles, the shaking hand, the poor eyesight and hearing. They just see the love in their grandparent's eyes."

Bob went on to tell of Mason and his mother's grief when her father died. He had been staying in this same health care center, and the family had come daily to visit with him. They had seen Bob in the hallway when they visited the grandfather and marveled at how much the two older men looked alike.

Bob told Norma that the boy had adopted him as his grandfather after his own grandfather had died.

"He comes every week," Bob said. "Sometimes twice a week."

He went on to explain that they shared the soda pop from Bob's little refrigerator or a piece of candy or a cookie.

As remarkable as Bob's resemblance is to Mason's grandfather, so too does Mason bear an uncanny likeness to Bob's own grandson. Bob's grandson is now grown and does not get to visit except on special holidays several times a year, so it is natural that these two, the young and the old, would reach out and adopt one another.

Bob's eyes glistened with tears when he said, "Sis, it's the secret of giving to one another. The Bible says, 'Every man shall give as he is able.' Mason and I are doing just that."

So is our sister Norma.

As she leaves my home this day, her bright red cloth bags litter my sitting room. She wraps her arms around me and gives me a hug that belies her seventy-eight years. Then she slides into her car and buckles her seat belt. She is already talking to her traveling companion as she pulls from my driveway.

—*Joan Watt*

I Always Have Time for You

I arrived late for the weekly first-sergeant council meeting hosted by our senior enlisted advisor, a grisly, no-nonsense air force chief master sergeant. As I took my seat in the middle of his weekly issues update, I couldn't ignore his focused stare. Once the meeting wound down, the chief asked me to stay behind. I knew he was unhappy. After giving me his spiel on punctuality and meeting etiquette, he asked me if I had anything to say.

Well, I've never been one to sugar-coat anything, so I figured, *What the heck, I'm already off his Christmas list; might as well tell it straight.*

"Chief," I said, "whenever a troop knocks on my door and asks me, 'First Sergeant, ya got a minute?' my answer will always be, 'Sure, come on in. I always have time for you.' Well, that's what happened this morning. Right before the meeting, a troop stopped by my office with a distressed look on his face and I knew he needed to talk."

Turns out he was having serious marital and financial problems, and when I'd asked him if he was thinking of suicide, he'd grown silent.

"Chief," I explained, "he immediately ratcheted up on my priority list. I just dropped him off at the chaplain's office, and I need to follow up right after this meeting."

For several seconds the chief stared at me, letting sink in what I had said. After a moment he replied, "Good call."

Nothing else was ever said about my being late. As with that meeting, I made it a point of never being late for a meeting without a good reason.

It wasn't a hard call for me. In fact, during the fourteen years I served as a first sergeant, "I always have time for you" was one of my most effective lines. It often opened the door to countless impromptu counseling and mentoring sessions—on the flight line, in hallways, break rooms, chow halls, wherever. I'd like to say that I came up with this philosophy all by myself, but I didn't; I learned it from the best.

On Christmas Day, December 25, 1990, our airbase in Saudi Arabia, not far from the Iraqi border, was honored with a visit by the legendary Bob Hope and his traditional Christmas show for military personnel serving in harm's way around the globe. Over the span of several decades, Mr. Hope had built a reputation as a generous, caring, and patriotic entertainer who effectively put politics and even his own personal safety aside to visit front-line troops and entertain them.

Several of the senior non-commissioned officers in our small unit, including myself, volunteered to cover the flight-line operations so that all the junior troops could attend the show. I would have loved to have seen it, but somehow making sure all the non com's caught the show seemed more important, so we missed it. Mr. Hope's specially painted and equipped Lockheed C-141 Starlifter was one of the planes we were charged with preparing for departure that day. He was scheduled to leave immediately after the show for another in-theater location to entertain even more troops.

When his departure time approached, I hoped to catch a glimpse of the legendary entertainer. Just as the aircraft's flight engineer and I were climbing out from under the wheel well, the entourage arrived. Mr. Hope and his wife Delores worked their way through the troops and some press members who had gathered at the aircraft to see him off.

The then eighty-seven-year-old living legend made his way to the aircraft and began climbing the stairs only a few feet from me. Seeing him sign several autographs, I frantically searched my pockets for a scrap of paper. All I could find was a single note of Saudi currency—a riyal note.

Without thinking, I shouted out, "Mr. Hope! Can I have an autograph?"

By then, he was on the top step of the boarding ladder looking tired and aged. His watchful wife shook her head and said, "No, no. Bob's very tired, and we have to be going."

To that, before my disappointment could even register, Bob Hope answered in a loud and cheerful voice, saying "Sure! I've always got time for you! That's why I'm here."

He came back down the ladder, took the note from my hand, and signed it. Then, to my surprise, he put his arm over my shoulder and led me away from the aircraft and the crowd. When we were alone, he asked me my name, how I was doing, and where I was from. He wanted to know about my wife and my three small daughters back home, and for about five minutes, he took a genuine interest in me and my well-being. He finished by telling me how much he admired and appreciated me and all the troops there. Then, looking me in the eyes, he told me to be careful and come home soon. With that, he made his way back to the aircraft and up the ladder, then turned and waved.

I composed myself and, remembering the insta-matic camera in my hand, snapped a quick shot of Mr. Hope just before he disappeared into the air-craft. Soon, the engines started, and I marshaled the aircraft out to the runway. As it turnèd away, I tearfully swelled with pride and saluted. I cannot tell you how special his words were to me and the terrific boost to my morale he provided.

The whole episode was special, of course, but most significant to me was the aged and obviously exhausted entertainer's declaration, "I always have time for you." How easy it would have been for him to have yielded to his wise and caring wife's urging to board the plane and get some rest before the next stop. Instead, Bob Hope put me, a stranger, before his own needs and desires. With a simple gesture and a few moments of his time, he touched me like no one else had and taught me all I needed to know about service before self.

—*Wm. Scott Hubbartt*

Angels Afoot

Like most children, I took my parents for granted. It wasn't until I became an adult that I realized their desire to make a difference in the lives of others was more than a personal choice; it was an innate part of their personalities. Frank and Millie Ricard performed their angel magic with neither fanfare nor a desire for recognition, which is perhaps why it took so long for me to appreciate and honor it. Because their kindness to others was something I accepted as a matter of course, I might never have evaluated this aspect of their personalities were it not for an event that my mother mentioned in passing.

We were sharing a glass of wine on my back deck, chatting about myriad things as mothers and daughters do, and she commented on this particular occurrence only as a bridge from one topic to another. I, on the other hand, saw it as a sprinkling of my parents' angel magic in its truest form, and I prodded her with questions, seeking details for a story I sensed was important.

Mama laughed at me and waved her hand as if to say, *Anyone would have done the same.*

But she was wrong, and I have never forgotten the story she told me that day.

Arizona in July is synonymous with brutal heat, boasting temperatures that soar well over 100 degrees. It also signals the onset of monsoon season, which was in full swing and just that morning had battered the Southern Arizona desert with severe thunder, lightning, rain, and high winds. Mama and Daddy opted to spend the day wandering the dry, air-conditioned mall, having a bite to eat, and taking in a movie. It seemed a nice way to spend a Saturday afternoon while leaving the storm outdoors.

They chose a casual restaurant for lunch and were perusing the menu when their waitress, a young woman in her mid-twenties, approached the table to introduce herself and take their beverage order. Mama and Daddy noted that her hair, drawn back in a ponytail, was damp, as were her clothes. She was friendly but distracted and seemed, they noted, to be quite frazzled.

Drawing her into conversation, they learned she was a single mother and a college student working two jobs. That particular day had been unkind to her. Her car broke down, forcing her to walk to work in the pummeling rain and wind. She was preoccupied with concerns about how being without a vehicle would affect her ability to care for her daughter as well as the added issue of simply affording vehicle repair and money for required college books. Her frustration was obvious, and the day's events had certainly left her in a certain amount of despair. Yet, her comments centered on ideas for solving her problems rather than complaining about them. Her attitude pricked my parents' interest.

They used their dining time to joke with the young lady and to entice smiles and laughs. They noted that she brightened when asked questions about her little girl, and Daddy conversed with her about her coursework at the University of Arizona, from which he had obtained a degree in psychology many years prior.

When Mama and Daddy finished with lunch, they said goodbye to their waitress and wished her well. Her plight and attempt at a positive attitude touched them, and they wondered what they might do to help.

They had time before the movie started to do some window shopping, and their meandering eventually led them into a bookstore. While browsing, they came across a slim volume that discussed the presence of angels on Earth, and they immediately knew what they wanted to do. After purchasing the book, they withdrew money from the bank, tucked the bills inside the book, and put the book into a bag, which they delivered to the restaurant cashier along with the request that it be given to the waitress at first opportunity. No, they said, no need to take their names.

Like a pair of Santa's elves, they watched with anticipation from a distance as the young woman opened the bag and smiled at each other when she found their gift and began to cry. She glanced around for her benefactors, looked askance at the cashier who could only shrug, and clutched the book to her as if it were pure gold. Her anonymous angels, pleased with their sprinkling of magic, disappeared.

I asked my mother if they ever returned to the restaurant to tell the waitress that it was they who had eased her burden that day. She told me they did not. It was their desire to offer help that would neither brook a prideful refusal nor require any thanks. They offered the money with a book on visiting angels so the young lady would understand the spirit in which the gift was offered.

I have thought many times of that young woman and how her day changed course because of a kind deed performed by two people who had not set out to do anything more special than spend a pleasant afternoon at the mall. I imagine she suspected who her angels were, but of course she would never know for certain.

It has been more than a decade since my mother shared this story with me, and in that time, both of my parents have become heaven's angels. In mourning their loss, I have often wondered what impact their good deed had on that young woman's life. I like to believe that she moved on after that day with a renewed spirit of faith. Wherever she is, I hope she still remembers my mama and daddy—not for the money that helped to ease her burden but rather for their small act of kindness, with its simple message of hope: Despite the challenges and cruelties we may encounter, the world is yet blessed with human beings who care about others. God's angels are afoot. They walk among us, sprinkling their magic wherever they go.

—Lisa Ricard Claro

The Rubber Chicken Cure

It's a funny thing about cancer: People don't know what to say to you. They shuffle their feet. They look away. They mumble. They think you'll drop dead right in front of them.

Nearly eleven years ago, I was diagnosed with invasive lobular breast cancer. As I underwent surgery, radiation, and chemotherapy, I was slowly sucked into a long, dark tunnel of isolation, withdrawing emotionally, watching through a distant pane of glass as life went on. I could hear people talk; I saw them laugh and plan and enjoy life. But I couldn't quite connect with what was happening. And, even though loved ones tried to include me in whatever they were doing, there was an invisible barrier between us. My family was worried enough; my friends had no idea what I was going through. I felt very much alone.

Then one day I was invited to Camp Living Springs, a camp for adults who had cancer—any kind of cancer. I'd heard about camps for children with cancer or disabilities before, but never one for adults. This one was sponsored, financed, and run by the caring volunteers of the local hospital auxiliary and some of the hospital's medical staff. Although I don't know it for sure, I imagine the whole idea of a camp like this began with someone who had first-hand experience with cancer and what it does to the lives and emotions of most adults. Even if we feel fine physically, inside we feel vulnerable, insecure, and helpless, no longer grown up, but rather suddenly like children again. What better way to dismiss our fears and re-experience childhood than at a sleepover camp planned especially for us.

We were a mixed group waiting for the bus: old men, young men, people in ill-fitting wigs, people who looked perfectly healthy, elderly women, and young mothers. We chatted nervously, not quite sure what the fifty or so of us had signed up for or what we'd be doing. That was the last time we had any doubts.

Before we left, our auxiliary volunteers handed out blue canvas goodie bags containing everything a real camper would need: a goofy-looking hat, bubble stuff, a yoyo, a disposable camera, a T-shirt, and other necessities. Everyone was assigned a buddy from the auxiliary. Mine promptly became "Mom," although she wasn't much older than me or her other "children." I liked her. She had a nice smile and gave out hugs readily.

We left for camp, singing loudly to the accompaniment of someone who'd brought along a guitar, our songs rattling the bus windows as much as the bumpy road did. As we crossed the bridge over Tampa Bay, we magically left our homes and our worries behind. We were footloose, carefree kids again, ready for adventure.

Soon we entered the shady compound of the retreat. Wooden buildings surrounded us, most joined by covered walkways and oak trees dripping with Spanish moss. We were far from civilization. We could be as loud as we wanted to, and we often were.

Over the three days of camp, we let loose, celebrating a way out-of-season Mardi Gras, wearing ridiculous masks we'd made in the overflowing craft room. We were also taught to make not-so-nice noises with a straw and our elbows. (Who knew that the serious radiologist who watched over our annual mammograms could play "When the Saints Go Marching In" with the straw and her knee pit?) Quieter moments found us rocking in the old wooden chairs scattered on the deck, getting massages, walking down by the lake, or doing early morning tai chi. We ate in a dining hall and slept in dorms on crackling, plastic-covered bunk beds set up for the real children who usually slept there.

As the hours passed, we slowly began to reconnect with life and to rediscover the people we had been before cancer came into our lives: People who enjoyed whacking a rubber chicken around the play room. People who laughed when, in the middle of the night, a cat happily settled herself into the bed of the only woman freaked out by cats. People who madly blew clouds of bubbles at the Mardi Gras king and queen.

Much of the silliness was instigated by the doctor, nurse, and our support group facilitator. In fact, it was the doctor who started the rubber chicken on its airborne rounds when things got quiet one evening. And our facilitator? Nobody danced harder or did a better Macarena than she did. Our many volunteer moms watched out for us but also played with us, as moms often do. And, like good moms, they were even prepared for the rain that never came with board games and indoor things to do.

We hated to leave but knew that we couldn't stay at camp forever. There were treatments to be taken, jobs to be returned to, and families who needed us.

As I was lying on the lower bunk on the last morning, I looked up at the bed above me. There, scratched in the plywood that held the upper mattress, was a simple record of children who had come before: straight-edged hearts with sets of initials carved in the center, two jagged names joined with the words "Best Friends Forever," or simply a child's name. I wanted to add my own message to that piece of painted plywood. I wanted to say, "Mickey was here," to leave something permanent behind in the impermanent world that was now mine.

As it turned out, I didn't need to carve a lasting message for the world because I'm still here and enjoying every day with a new appreciation that was nurtured, teased, and giggled back to life at Camp Living Springs. I will always be grateful to those who took the time to provide me and many other adults with the chance to escape, really escape, from the uncertain world that had become our lives—and to whisk us away at no cost to us, so no one would be left behind. But more than that, I'm grateful to those caring people for giving me exactly what I needed when I needed it most: human connection at a time in my life when I felt completely alone.

—*Michele Ivy Davis*

If We Eat Less,
They Can Eat More

I don't know when my heart grew cold. Once, I'd had a passion for the world's hungry. In my twenties, I'd supported children in Africa and Central America, faithfully sending my twenty-five dollars a month and watching the child grow in the pictures the agency sent me. But at some point my benevolent steam ran out and I stopped sending the checks. Unmoved, I watched celebrities on television holding malnourished children and making pleas for money while the masses of starving villagers stood in the background like unidentifiable figures in a photo negative. Had I been overexposed to the world's hunger without being exposed at all? Hunger had no face for me. No one I knew was hungry, no mother I knew ever wondered how she'd feed her children the next day.

That I'd become numb to this suffering became clear to me one day as I listened to a friend. She spoke with anguish about her concern for the people of Darfur, their hunger and their suffering. I'd never witnessed such compassion.

I must go and see the face of hunger for myself, I thought. *That is the only way the eyes of my heart will be opened.*

My desire was met by the opportunity to go with a mission team to the rural, mountainous village of Ranquitte, Haiti. For one week, our group of six men and two women would build a house, make repairs in the compound, go on home visits, and we women, both nurses, would work in the medical clinic. After months of preparation, the day finally arrived for our departure.

As we rode in the trucks from the airport to the village, we were greeted by half-clothed children along the route, waving and yelling out *"Blanc! Blanc! Blanc!"* They chased after us in our wake of dust. Women passed by on their way home from the market, the old women riding on pack-laden mules and the younger ones balancing jugs of water on their heads. The smell of wood fires permeated the air as people cooked under their makeshift kitchen shelters. Young boys stopped playing their marble-like game with cashews when they heard the rare sound of automobile motors, standing up to observe the new group of foreigners.

When we neared the entrance of the mission, our team leader, who'd led groups to Ranquitte for years, yelled out to the guard to open the gate. "Po Po!" he greeted the guard and gave him a man-hug through the open window. "Good to see you, my friend."

We took a tour of the compound, which included a school, the medical clinic, agricultural project, and dormitory flanked by two residences for mission staff. The entire area was surrounded by a six-foot block wall that sloped down the mountainside. After we settled into our quarters, we walked next door to the founding mother's house, where we'd have all our meals.

Before we sat down, our team leader instructed us. "I want you to take what you need but don't put on your plate more than you'll eat. The ladies who prepared your food will eat what is left over."

I thought about that as I passed the bowl of beans and rice. *How well do they eat when the mission teams aren't here?* I wondered.

After a night of disrupted sleep from roosters crowing and men snoring in the next room, I awoke to the sound of singing. The women who cooked for us began each day with hymns. What a lovely contrast to the babble of morning talk shows at home. Later, when we sat down to pancakes slathered with peanut butter and syrup, I remembered what our team leader had told us the night before.

If I eat less, they can eat more, I thought as I resisted a second helping.

Following breakfast, the other nurse and I walked to the turquoise building that was the clinic. A Haitian nurse, dressed in a white uniform and white stockings like I wore thirty years ago, assigned us to exam rooms with our interpreters. She brought in my first patient, an elderly man with a machete cut to his ankle.

"It happened when he was working in his garden," my interpreter told me.

The old man sat down and placed his injured foot into the basin of antiseptic cleaner. The heat in the room, which had only one small window, was quickly building, and as I stooped down to clean his foot, perspiration ran down my back.

After I wrapped his wound with gauze, he stood, turned to me with a slight smile, and said, "*Merci*" as he tipped his head.

My next patient was a three-year-old girl who sat listless in her mother's arms. The child was amazingly clean and wearing a lacy white dress. Her mother described symptoms that became commonplace that morning: fever, abdominal pain, and lethargy. The lab tests confirmed that the girl had malaria and typhoid.

That day, and in the clinic days that followed, we saw a steady flow of patients, mostly mothers and grandmothers with children. The women had weary eyes and thin frames that seemed to bend under the weight of their lives. Many of the children had worms, and all were malnourished.

How awful it must be not to be able to feed your children, I thought as I considered my grown sons, healthy and always with food to eat.

In the afternoons, our team went on home visits. The mayor of Ranquitte had chosen some of their most needy families for us. We loaded backpacks with beans, rice, children's multivitamins, clothes, and children's treat bags filled with toys and hygiene items. We headed out with an interpreter, as well as a band of young men and boys who had nothing better to do than follow us around.

The family compounds had two or three huts, most made of sticks and mud, the nicer ones made of concrete block. Around fifteen people altogether lived in each compound. Some families had a pig or cow tied to a rope, but more often they had a few goats. Occasionally, a couple of chickens ran about the yard. All the animals were bony.

We stood outside the home as the family huddled together around the doorway. The parents listened when our designated spokesperson told the family who we were and that we were visiting on behalf of the mission. During some visits, we did impromptu health checks, bandaging wounds and helping with simple ailments. At one home we showed the children how to blow up balloons and then played with them, tapping the shiny red orbs to their happy cries.

At the end of each visit, an interpreter would ask the parents how many children they had who were old enough for the chewable vitamins. He demonstrated how to open the medicine bottle and emphasized that the vitamins were to help the children "grow big and strong." After handing the parents the food, clothes, and vitamins, we gave the children their treat bags. The parents responded with a bashful "*Merci*," and the children smiled happily as they pulled the toys from their bags.

A young man named Johnson accompanied us as our interpreter on many of the home visits. When we waited between houses due to downpours, he studied for his national exams, which would determine if he'd be promoted to the next level at school. I touched his shoulder once to get his attention and was startled by the feel of boney sharpness that had been hidden by his baggy shirt.

One afternoon, Johnson walked alongside the other nurse at the rear of our caravan and spoke to her quietly out of earshot of the others. "Do you think I could have a bottle of the vitamins? I don't get much to eat."

We'd heard he was one of seven children. At nineteen, he'd been telling the parents of small children how they'd grow big and strong from the vitamins, all the while hungry himself. She gave him the vitamins.

As we neared the end of our week, we were making one of our final home visits and had to run for cover at the boom of thunder. The family motioned all twelve of us into their mud hut. We stood shoulder to shoulder as the wind whipped the banana palms and a driving rain pinged loudly on the tin roof. The head of the household was a bent old woman who hobbled around with a limp as she pulled out plastic chairs and insisted we sit down. After almost an hour, the rain slowed to the point that we were able to hear. It was my turn to be our spokesperson.

"Thank you for giving us shelter in your home," I said to the woman, who looked at me intently with her crinkly golden eyes. Had I seen her in the clinic? Somehow, she seemed familiar to me. "We're from the United States and came here to serve at the mission." I went on to ask her if she knew the work of the clinic and school.

The little lady seemed to be taking in every word as Johnson interpreted. A big smile spread across her face and she sprang from her chair, clapped her hands, and danced around in a circle. Then, she spoke rapidly, her hands raised in the air.

Johnson chuckled as he watched her and interpreted. "She says that she loves God and that she and her family are so glad we came to her home!"

We finished our visit and told the family goodbye. I carefully made my way down the muddy slope behind her house, but the lady, barefoot and agile, caught up to me.

"For you," she said and handed me an enamel cup with five brown eggs.

I looked into her eyes, shining with love, and then down at the eggs. How could she give me such a huge gift when she had so little? The eggs would be one of the few sources of protein for her family. Tears streamed down my face. Overwhelmed by her generosity, her cup of gratitude, I hugged the little lady and said, "Thank you. *Merci*. Thank you very much."

I turned to go down the hill, but Johnson stopped me. "She says she needs her cup back." He smiled at her.

Of course, I thought and nodded my head, remembering the sparseness of her home. The pretty cup, trimmed with a blue rim and bouquets of flowers, would be missed. Smiling, I took the five brown eggs and carefully placed them inside the bags of clothes. I gave her a hug and waved goodbye to her family.

We finished our home visits, saw our last patients in the clinic, and said tearful goodbyes to our interpreters and the mission staff. It seemed like we were just getting started when it was time to leave. We were mostly quiet on the long trip home, occasionally sharing memories from our week.

Over the next days and months, I thought often of Ranquitte. I'd look at the clock and think, *They'd be closing the clinic for lunch now.* In my mind's eye, I could see the school and the students milling around outside before class, the adolescent girls in their bright plaid skirts and neatly braided hair, the boys in their white shirts and blue pants. I found myself going to our globe and touching the small country of Haiti.

I can make a difference there, I thought as I sat down to a supper of beans and rice. *If I eat less they can eat more,* I reasoned as I wrote out my first check for the mission. Hunger now had a face for me. It was the old man nodding with his gentle smile, and the three-year-old with the lacy white dress, and Johnson carrying a bottle of multivitamins. It was the lady with the crinkly golden eyes handing me a cup of eggs. Yes, the egg lady of Ranquitte showed me that compassion has a huge price, but it has a far greater reward.

—Connie Rosser Riddle

The Sweetest Gift

"Mom, do we have a cake mix I can use?"

"I think so. Check the cupboard, in the back. What are you making?"

"Cupcakes. A kid at school has a birthday."

Lisa is so nice to her friends, I thought.

My thirteen-year-old daughter remembers birthdays, makes people cards when they are sick, and sends encouraging notes written in colored gel pens in her neat, artistic hand. She is my middle child, the one most likely to blend in, becoming invisible, according to the books I'd read on birth-order. Not this kid; the authors obviously had never met Lisa.

She was the one most likely to get lost, though, especially when she was little. She would fall asleep on the living room floor on the far side of the sofa or on a throw rug at the back of the coat closet, and no amount of frantic calling would wake her.

Or she would disappear, only to be found investigating artwork in a neighbor's garden or climbing to the top of a high fence and getting stuck there, not that she would admit she couldn't climb down by herself. Neighbors were called more than once to search for our little explorer. "Careful" was not in her vocabulary. Fiercely independent, she once scaled the shelves of her closet—and fell, needing stitches in her forehead—rather than ask for help in getting a toy off the top shelf. She had her own ideas on clothes, as well, wearing her favorite red velvet dress and white lace tights even in the heat of July.

Lisa's personality remained constant as she grew into this eighth-grader, a beautiful, long-limbed colt with braces on her teeth. Blue jeans replaced frilly dresses and patent leather Mary Janes gave way to Nikes, but Lisa stayed the same, my kind yet passionate daughter. She was still my explorer and still calibrated her compass to her own true north. And today my sweet girl had taken it upon herself to make cupcakes for one of her friends. I was so proud.

Have you ever fallen and had the breath knocked out of you? Hit so hard you think you'll never draw air into your lungs again? That's how the vice principal's call hammered me when I answered the phone the next day. Vice principals do not call unless there is trouble. He assured me Lisa was okay, and I let out the breath I didn't know I'd been holding.

"I called to tell you that in twenty years of teaching I have never seen anything like what Lisa did today," he said.

I held my breath again as I thought, My Lisa? My sweet daughter? He must have the wrong kid. What could she have done?

My silence prompted him to go on. "I've never seen a student do anything so nice for anyone who needed it more."

Wait, this was good. Why was the vice principal calling me with good news?

"What did she do?" I asked.

He explained to me about the cupcakes.

When Lisa came home from school that afternoon, I told her the vice principal from her school had phoned me.

"Yeah," she answered. "I got called out of math class to go to his office. Everyone thought I was in trouble, but he just wanted to know what was going on at lunch."

"What did you tell him?"

"Well, I told him how Cody, Tyler, Ashley, and I had this club and we were trying to think of a project we could do. I had the idea of pairing up together and sitting with people at lunch who were eating by themselves. This was a couple of weeks ago."

Lisa and Ashley had sat with a boy who is in special education classes. They got to talking about birthdays, and Lisa asked Jordan when his birthday was. He told them it was coming up but that he lives in a group home and they don't celebrate birthdays there.

"I remembered his birthday was today, so I made the cupcakes yesterday," Lisa explained. "Ashley brought a two-liter of soda and some birthday cups, plates, and napkins left over from her little brother's party, and we got some other kids together at lunch today to sing 'Happy Birthday' to Jordan. That's when the vice principal came over—he's always patrolling at lunch—and asked what we were doing, I just said we were having a party for Jordan, and he left, but then later I got called over the PA system to go to his office."

The vice principal wanted to know why they had a birthday party for Jordan at school. Lisa's explanation about her Bible club's project and the group home and making cupcakes left the vice principal speechless.

"He just shook his head, took off his glasses, and rubbed his eyes," Lisa told me. "Finally, he said he was going to call my parents but that I wasn't in trouble, he was proud of what I did, and I could go back to math."

I blinked back tears, picturing the only birthday celebration this boy would get this year, maybe the only one for many years. I remembered my own junior high days and how cruel some of the kids were to anyone who was different. Although I was not overtly mean, I certainly had not attempted to reach out to the unpopular kids. I had lacked the courage to make myself vulnerable by befriending the weird kids, the ones who existed at the periphery of the fragile social structure, the ones who ate lunch alone. I would not have even known how. My wise daughter knew how; all it took was cupcakes and one adventurous, independent, kind spirit.

—*Betsy McPhee*

Where Magic Lives

The little girl knew exactly where magic lives, in what word and what land. She might sit beside you and impishly challenge you to guess this secret magic.

"Hmmmm," the grownup might muse. "Could it be 'abracadabra?' 'Shazam?' Perhaps 'supercalifragilisticespialadocious?'"

Giggling, the child would shake her head vigorously and then give a clue, saying that the magic word and the magic land have one and the same name.

"Oh, I see," the adult might say. "Well, then, could it be Oz? . . . No? Then Narnia? . . . No? Disneyland?"

The giggles would ensue again as the child, her black eyes dancing and her curls bouncing, shook her head "no" once more. For the guesses were not even close.

The little girl knew exactly where magic lay, in what word and what land. She was so sure of its place that she often wondered if it even existed when she was not there. It seemed far too enchanted and wonderful to be an everyday place; perhaps it simply peeked out from the fog now and then to lend color to an otherwise ordinary world.

She knew when she was there because the flat, sandy land of her own world suddenly turned to rolling hills shaded by hundreds of welcoming trees and the soil to something red and rich. She knew when she was there because there was a different look, a different feel, a magic in the air. Nothing was the same there, not even the sounds and smells. Not that anything was wrong with her own world, but here everything was tinged with magic. And that was odd, because none of the motifs of fairy tales applied. Or did they? Oh, the child was quite sure they did. Enchantment had simply rendered them a different form.

The castle sat far down a twisty, dirt road sprinkled with fairy dust and lined on either side with black-eyed Susans, like sentries. Of course, the castle was enchanted, so it did not particularly look like the castles of fairy tales. It was quite simple—a tiny white farmhouse really, smoke curling from its chimney and guarded by its keeper, Old Ring. Upon the child's arrival, Old Ring rushed out, a blur of brown and white barking terror—until, of course, he recognized who dared enter the kingdom and the bark turned to welcome.

Fairy godmothers? Oh, yes! Not just one, but four of them! And a loving old Papa magician as well!

The little girl knew exactly where magic lay, in what word and in what land.

When I was a girl, I knew a word for "magic." And the word was also a magical place. The place was magic because it was the cradle of all things wonderful, all things comforting, all things imaginable that could make a little girl feel loved and adored. The feel was wrapped up in so many things; it was quite impossible to tell what exactly was magic about it. The smell of good things wafting from an iron stove? The aunts who stopped their bustling to wrap the girl in great bear hugs? The twinkling fireflies across the fields? The Pa who leaned across the oilcloth-covered great table, brown eyes twinkling, as he teased her? The sound of whippoorwills and crickets? Or was it the final enveloping hug when she sank at the end of a day into a warm, soft feather bed? Impossible to say.

But the magic word and the magic place were one and the same: Tennessee. When I was a girl, it was magic.

And when I was a young woman, struggling to make a home, struggling to carve out a career, struggling to raise children, it was magic then, too. Now and then, stresses would pile up, deep and thick, like the trees of a horrid troll's forest. And always one place would come to mind that I could go back to and then come home from refreshed: Tennessee.

The word and the place were magic for my own children, too. I would bundle them into a car, and we would traipse the long way. The farmhouse was gone and so was Pa, but the aunts were the same and their homes were the same. They would greet us with eyes dancing and laughter on their lips, envelop us in great hugs, and for a space of time, we would bask in their magic. I would get welcome relief and be urged to go explore the old places with an uncle. My children would greet me at my return, the telltale pink sticky around their lips telling me they had raided their great-aunts' strawberries, the smiles on their faces telling me they knew the same magic I knew.

I still go back, as I always will. But it is not the same, and the reasons for going are different. My uncles are gone. We lost two of those loving aunts last year; two remain. I do not go these days to find the magic, though I find it in the two aunts that remain just the same. They are very old now, ancient with years and experiences, but their eyes light up like I remember. They are too frail to embrace me in great bear hugs anymore and I am careful when I hug them because they are so thin and fragile, but I feel the magic in the soft embrace. They cannot fix the "great spreads" they once did, and I bring them treats they do not often see in the nursing home that cares for them. They cannot shop for themselves, and so I sit beside them and make a list and bring back to them what they wish.

The last time I was there, the bright eyes of one of those aunts followed me as I bustled about the room, folding and putting away freshly laundered clothing, organizing drawers and closets. Twisting in her wheelchair, she turned to my husband.

"She is like Mama," she said. "She stays busy, just like Mama."

I heard what she said and thought briefly of the grandmother I never knew. As I continued my business—watering a plant, straightening the bedspread, adjusting curtains—I heard the soft voice speak again.

"She even looks like Mama."

That's when I knew: we have come full circle.

When I was a child, they were my magic—my comfort, my color in a very ordinary world. When I was a struggling young adult, they were my magic—my relief from daily stress, my place to go home to when life overwhelmed. Now they look forward to my visits as color in an ordinary world and would have me there every minute I can spare from my own world.

Their mama took care of them once, very long ago, and they are in need of care again. And it is my turn to repay what was given to me. I was proud to hear that elderly aunt I love so pronounce me "like mama." For no one on Earth could have loved her more, with the same warmth and total giving as her Mama long ago. I could not possibly replace "Mama," but something about what I could give them reminded them of her. Somehow, I was returning the comfort given me for so many years. It felt good to know it was so, that it was possible, that I might make a bit of "magic" for my aunt as she had so often made for me.

Full circle. We all come full circle. Then there comes a time to repay the comforts we have basked in, the pleasures we have enjoyed, and the kindnesses we have been shown. We accept these gifts graciously; for a while we do not question the sacrifices that made them possible. But there comes a day when we realize we must give back what has been given. We come full circle. It is the way of life, and it is a good thing. It is magic.

—*Jan Philpot*

All It Takes Is an Open Heart

The photograph shows a handsome young man in uniform, his smile shining from a sincere face. Beside him stands the sixth President of Ireland, Patrick Hillery. The photograph was taken in the late 1970s, when Ireland was in a deep recession and the oil crisis raged, but that failed to diminish the optimism and open heart of the young man who had just received a medal for his volunteer Red Cross work.

Many years later, I was lucky enough to gain that young man as my father-in-law, Tom. He welcomed me into his family with an open heart. My new husband had told me the story of how Tom had lost his father at the age of fourteen. In a family of two boys and one girl, all still in school, Tom, the younger son, stepped forward to leave his education and run the family's grocery store. It was a huge responsibility for a boy to assume, but it enabled his older brother to continue studying and become a pharmacist.

Tom ran the family business with great acumen and fairness until his mother died. Then he moved town with his own young family of three boys, later creating a new business with the eldest of them, which thrives to this day. This much I knew.

I would happily have given him another medal for being a good father, father-in-law, and outstanding grandfather to my own two children. His wonderful, laughter-filled company raised my spirits each time I saw him, so I was deeply confused to find the family in uproar on one visit because he had been nominated for the Person of the Year Award. As a recent member of the family, I stifled my own view rather than blurt out, "But why shouldn't he get that? He does endless errands for the residents in the homeless shelter, and he's a respected local businessman. He's a good guy."

As I listened, I learned that he had also been nominated for his unpaid work helping the legal system as a Justice of the Peace (somewhat like a lay attorney) and for helping a troubled young man to find work and friendship when he'd been at his lowest ebb. And those errands and handyman tasks he did for the homeless shelter? That was because he didn't want the shelter to fall into disrepair after he'd spent years fund-raising for, designing, and mentoring it through various regulatory hoops. Without Tom, that haven for the less fortunate would never have existed. Since it opened, he'd dedicated countless volunteer hours working at a national level to coordinate charitable organizations to create homes for those who otherwise would never have a roof over their heads. I got a real education on helping out that day at the kitchen table while the family debated the nomination.

Finally Tom spoke, "I'm going to ask the newspaper editor to remove my name from the short list. I don't like asking for a favor, but it's not fair. Plenty of other people helped me with the shelter."

I couldn't believe he was refusing the award. He had done amazing work; why shouldn't he be proud of it? I've since realized that his innate modesty prevented him from taking credit for any of his quiet charitable achievements. He wanted to help and didn't need acknowledgement.

Five years later, I did the hardest job of my life when Tom lost his battle with cancer. I had to tell my children that the grandfather they adored was gone. Then we had to rush to my husband's hometown for the funeral.

As the only family member with young children, I'd been spared most of the endless weeks of bedside despair, but now I had to explain that Tom, one of the most vital people you could ever meet, wouldn't be coming home from the hospice. How do you tell preschoolers that news? I said the words as kindly as I could, with my arms wrapped tightly around them. The concept had no meaning for them, but they knew I was upset, and despite my best efforts, they asked many times on the journey if they would get to visit their grandfather at the hospital. Each time, it unleashed my tears again. They'd loved the kindness of the nurses and getting a wave from their grandfather, who'd used precious energy to communicate his love to them during his illness.

The following days passed in shock and sadness. Having been unable to stand witness to his final hours, I talked to anyone who had known him and gathered a clearer picture of the man I'd loved for a brief decade. As his wife unearthed photographs of his younger life, the stories flowed and I stored them in my heart and memory. My son whistled with admiration when he heard his grandfather had been a volunteer firefighter. He and other brave men had dropped their businesses when the bell rang and run toward the flames, rather than away. During the dark days of an earlier recession he, along with others, had collected enough funding to start a cooperative steel foundry in their town, which provided jobs for nearly thirty years.

Random strangers arrived at the various funeral ceremonies and told us their stories. Many had been unheard by the family until that day.

"He taught me how to ride a bike," smiled one lady in her sixties. "I was terrified and my father had given up trying. Tom brought me to a quiet, flat lane and kept encouraging me until I managed it."

My mother-in-law recalled the number of times Tom had arrived home on Christmas Eve to announce that she'd need to make the turkey stretch to another plate or two. He couldn't bear to think of someone spending Christmas alone. He'd issue invitations to the most unlikely characters, but it always made for an entertaining dinner table.

A beautiful wreath and letter arrived from a woman Tom had mentored early in her career and treated like his own daughter. I could understand her grief and fond memories. I'd felt he was my extra father, too.

A besuited young man with his youngsters by the hand arrived to sympathize with the family. He explained to Tom's widow that her husband had repeatedly helped him to sober up, reconcile with his parents, and keep away from drugs. He cried as he told her the story, as his children looked up in amazement. Tom had never even mentioned this to his wife, whom he had known since childhood.

He worked silently, constantly, and changed a thousand lives.

We've another photograph of an older Tom, with our eighth and current president, Mary McAleese, laughing by his side. It was taken at the opening day of an assisted-living apartment complex for the elderly, again shepherded to fruition by Tom. Although he didn't get a medal that day, his smile lights the whole frame. The two photographs give a glimpse into a lifetime dedicated to helping others.

Tom's sons have been asked to take their father's role in local charity work, but nobody is ready to sit in his chair at the table. Between them, his family coaches local football teams, cares for seriously ill relatives, and gives many hours to their communities. None of them will accept a Person of the Year Award anytime soon. Tom taught them well, in the only way that counts, by example.

As for me, I'll teach my children to honor Tom's memory by volunteering themselves. We've already cleaned our local beach and we've replaced rubbish with trees and flowers. I understand now that anybody can make a difference, if they have an open heart.

—Grace Tierney

Of Worth and Grace

In the dubious privacy of his officer barracks, the captain leaned back on his bunk's woolen blanket and grunted. An energetic and upcoming air force flight surgeon, he'd grown used to others making unreasonable demands.

Opposite him slumped the unit's middle-aged chaplain, gnarled fingers clenched, head drooped a little forward. Anxious. Uncertain. Aware of the imposition of his request but desperate enough to ask anyway.

"How many are we dealing with?" Cap asked, smacking his lips softly. His muscular forearms bunched as he sipped cheap whiskey from a tin cup.

"Too many."

No real surprise there. Again Cap grunted. "Supplies?"

"Some."

Right. Government supplies couldn't be used on civilians, and local supplies were thin on the ground. Cap raised an eyebrow.

The chaplain's head dipped further. "Few."

"Yeah." In other words, he'd be working with a wing and a prayer, expected to fix a world of woes with one small soggy bandage. He already worked Monday to Saturday. This would mean giving up his precious Sunday, taking a bitterly cold hour and a half drive into mountains, then working until it was too dark to see for the sole purpose of doing a good deed.

Cap shook his head slightly and took a deep swig from his mug. He already knew he'd agree. Damn war. The orphans needed and deserved his help, and he wasn't about to leave them hanging.

"Yeah, okay. Set it up," he grumbled.

In a world gone mad, what was one more thankless act? The whiskey burned its way down his gullet, reminding him he was still alive in this hell-hole, dulling for a moment the smell of dust and desperation and death.

At 5:30 A.M. the next Sunday, as he bounced over a rough dirt road in an ancient, drab blue school bus, Cap cursed his decision. Dead winter. Even in his full arctic, military-issue woolens, he shivered, wishing he was back snug in his bed.

Beside him sat a fighter pilot and mechanical engineer. The guy was tops in his field, yet when he heard what Cap was up to, he had offered to tag along. "Even if I just carry your bag, Doc," he'd said in an earnest voice. It was hard not to admire that level of humility and service.

On the other side sat a nun, who, at only twenty-seven years old, was a registered nurse and pharmacist, spoke seven languages, and was a real life angel. She'd combined her two afternoons a month off so she could help. Their meager medical supplies rested in her lap: a small cardboard box of bandages, antiseptic, and antibacterial and antifungal cream. No drugs, nothing sophisticated. This would be cowboy medicine at best; round them up and try to head them in the right direction with little more than good intentions.

Clothing, food, and bedding packed the rest of the bus—simple things people back home took for granted but were in short supply in many of the local orphanages. The injustice bit harder than the cold.

"Check this!" called the driver, jarring Cap from his reverie.

They'd turned into the orphanage. Cap pressed his nose to the cold fogged glass, not believing what he saw. Throngs of kiddies clad only in cheap running suits and sandshoes lined both sides of the street. Not even any socks. Their tiny toes and tushes must have been frozen, yet there they stood, smiling their welcome and waving enthusiastically, like he was the King of Siam. He only hoped he could do something to warrant the fanfare.

When the bus stopped, the fighter pilot excused himself to go fix things around the complex—an outdoor well pump, hinges on doors, general maintenance. No job was too small or too simple for him, a glowing example of what a great man can be.

Cap set up clinic in a small bare room with a seemingly endless stream of little patients lined in front of the door, coughing and shuffling. Sore throats, skin infections, rashes, dental problems . . . the list was endless. One doctor to more than two hundred kids; it was a daunting task.

Halfway through the exhausting day, Cap looked up to see a sweet three-year-old standing quietly at the door, her eyes huge and intent, watchful. She didn't move until directed. Once the nun beckoned her in, the girl scurried to stand before Cap, still silent. Cap frowned as he looked down on her swollen and obviously infected tear gland. She risked losing her eye without treatment and it had to be painful, but he had no local anesthetic and no antibiotics to help her. She needed an ophthalmic surgeon, not a flight surgeon with only a knife and an alcohol wipe.

A concerned glance at the nun met with understanding. He heaved a sigh. It was him and his knife or nothing. Both the nun and the child put their trust in him as their only hope.

The nun called the little girl into her lap. Quickly, she explained that Cap needed to cut her to drain the bad things from her eye.

"It will hurt, but you mustn't move," the nun warned her softly.

Little dark eyes flicked from the nun to Cap as he prepared to lance the abscess. He swallowed hard at the bravery of this small child. A stranger with a knife was coming at her eye, and yet she didn't move, did not even cry out when he cut her. He drained the infection as best he could, ever aware she felt each movement. The nun cleaned and dressed the eye. Still, the tot did not cry. She stood and listened to care instructions, then backed out of the room bowing. The faith, respect, and gratitude shown by that small, helpless child hit Cap like a thunderbolt. His throat too closed with emotion for words, he looked back to the nun and her angelic smile, knowing she felt it, too.

Three days later, Cap returned to check on his patient. The orphanage *mamasan* led him up the winding path to the hut on top of the hill. With coal furnaces under the floor, it was a warmer place to wait. Very soon little footsteps pattered, running up the path. The small girl stopped at the door and removed her shoes, then darted across the room, dove into his arms, and kissed his cheek. She beamed at him. Her eye was open, the infection all but gone, and the look on her face one of joy and gratitude.

Cap's heart swelled. He knew he'd just been paid more for services rendered than top Beverly Hills surgeons. In the midst of war and ugliness, he'd witnessed a little miracle—one worth every-thing. Worth facing the bitter cold winter's morning. Worth sacrificing his only day off that week. Worth all the time he'd spent in medical school.

"We were all of us blessed," he told me, his voice still choked. "I knew that if I never did anything else in my life, if all I had was that moment, then my life has been worthwhile."

The humbling memory stayed with Cap and helped make him the fine man and doctor he is to this day. Though he's had many successes and achievements since that winter of 1976 in South Korea, that kiss on his cheek remains the pure gold in his life's treasure chest, a permanent infusion of worth and grace.

—*Lyndell King*

Beyond the Classroom

Mark was a great kid from a bad neighborhood. A scholarship fund provided his tuition to Catholic High, where he contributed—and not in a small way—to the sports program. On the football field he showed considerable talent, running the ball past the opposition and even jumping a mound of fellow players to make the touchdown. But it was a mound of a different sort that showcased Mark's greatest talent: he was a pitcher. In his junior year, scouts from pro baseball teams lined the bleachers right alongside the college coaches. His pitch of 85 to 95 miles an hour and excellent strikeout stats had made Mark a much sought-after recruit.

Mark struggled in the classroom, though. He was plenty bright, just behind, perhaps due to a more than difficult home environment. Mark's mom died from a drug overdose while he was in high school. I remember the funeral and watching Mark cry as he hung his head over the casket. He left to live with an elderly grandmother.

The area where Mark's grandmother lived was dangerous, and he was soon the victim of a drive-by shooting. The school community jumped to his aid, working behind the scenes almost immediately. While the ambulance sped away, a student's dad who was a surgeon accepted Mark as his patient. He met the ambulance at the hospital and whisked Mark away to surgery, removing the bullet and then making arrangements for therapy so that Mark's muscles could be retrained. Another family, whose son Kevin also attended Catholic High and played sports, fixed a bedroom for Mark. Kevin and Mark became best friends, and Kevin's dad took a personal interest in Mark, even attending parent/teacher conferences with him.

I met Mark in my resource room. At first, his teachers sent practice sets and homework for me to help him complete. When I had a better idea of his needs, I began remedial tutoring so that we could address the gaps in his education.

Despite the attention from pro scouts, Mark had made up his mind that he wanted to attend college. Interest from several universities was high, but Mark's scores on his college entrance exams were low. Somehow, some way, he had to make better marks on his ACT.

Several teachers discussed Mark's needs. We agreed that he required help far beyond what we could offer him within the time constraints of our class periods. After-school tutoring wasn't possible because of football and/or baseball practice. Some felt Mark should give up sports and concentrate on "schooling." But, in reality, his opportunity to attend college was linked to sports; so to miss practice and then perform any less than at his best on the field was counterproductive.

A fellow teacher, Mrs. Jones, offered to tutor Mark in math at her home. I scheduled Mark to come to my house for all other areas of the test. No one paid us. Mrs. Jones summed it up this way: "Pay day doesn't always come on Mondays."

When we were not working with Mark to improve his skills for the ACT, the coach and Kevin's dad took him to various colleges to talk with both baseball and football program coaches. He settled on the one college that offered him scholarships to play both sports. As you might expect, we were all elated but a little concerned. If Mark did not score the ACT minimum required by that university, he could not attend, no matter how talented he was.

The day came for Mark to take the ACT. I picked him up and took him for breakfast, then delivered him to the testing center, along with pencils, candy bars, and apples supplied by his other teachers.

It takes months to receive the results of college entrance exams—so long, in fact, that I lost my sense of when to begin expecting Mark's scores. One afternoon after school, while grading papers in my room, I heard quite a commotion outside the door. It sounded like a freight train coming down the hall. Then suddenly the freight train burst through my door.

Mark lifted me out of the seat behind my desk, spun me around in the air, and jubilantly yelled over and over, "I'm going to college! I'm going to college! I'm going to college!"

"I guess you got your scores?" I asked once he set me down.

"Well, *yeah!*" he laughed. "And guess what? It is one point more than I need to be accepted. One point extra! Thank you, thank you, thank you! Now, where's Mrs. Jones? I've got to tell her too!"

And the freight train was off and running again.

Until that moment, I had never quite understood, *Pay day doesn't always come on Mondays.* But the meaning became clear the instant Mark ran into the room to announce his news. No amount of money could ever replace my spin in the air at the hands of a boy who finally had a chance at a better life.

Sometimes we educators get stuck in a rut, feeling we are limited by the walls of our rooms. And sometimes we are. But there are those times when a special circumstance dictates a different path, one that requires the involvement of a community. Speaking of adages, here's another: *It takes a village to raise a child.* There's some wisdom in that one, for sure.

—Eloise Elaine Schneider

Fixing a Faucet while
Mending a Soul

About five months after my husband Steve died, I woke up to the maddening sound of a dripping faucet coming from my kitchen. I knew it needed a washer—at least, that's what I surmised. The truth is, I didn't know what it needed because I didn't know how to fix a faucet—or anything else, for that matter. It wasn't a gender issue; I had plenty of women friends who could wield a hammer and a pair of pliers with the best of them, and I admired their prowess. But that kind of thing just wasn't my forte. When it came to screwdrivers, I didn't know a Philips from a standard, and my idea of a nut driver (another type of screwdriver) was someone who couldn't control his or her road rage.

In the twenty-five-year partnership between Steve and me, I had been the "creative" one. A writer and an entertainer, I brought the same inventive inclination I used in my work to our home. It was I who painted and papered the walls and ceilings and converted thrift-store bargains into objects d'art with decoupage and stencils. Steve was the "practical" one. He was an accountant by profession, but he also had a marvelous knack for knowing how to repair everything in the house without ever having to call on a professional.

Steve had been bedridden for eight months during his last illness, and I had been his sole caregiver. During that time, my focus changed dramatically. Whereas I had once been keenly aware of my surroundings—tending the nest that I had cultivated and adorned with love and care throughout our shared life—when he was ill, I was no longer aware of anything other than my husband and the precious time we had left together. I certainly wasn't paying attention to leaky faucets.

For months after he passed, I was still oblivious to such things. I was overwhelmed with grief. I admit that I was also angry that a man who was so good should have his life cut short prematurely. But that dripping faucet roused me somewhat from my pity party of one and reminded me that I had been neglecting the house badly. The gutters hadn't been cleaned for over a year. The dishwasher door required adjusting, and a light fixture in the hallway needed to be replaced. Now that Steve was gone, I felt more vulnerable and wanted to have new deadbolt locks installed. I had yet to put together a bookcase I'd ordered from a catalogue. It had been advertised as being "easy to assemble." Easy for who? I couldn't get past the first shelf.

What I needed was a handyman who didn't mind tackling small chores. I wrote down a list of all the things that needed mending and attending, opened the Yellow Pages, and looked for someone who was licensed, bonded, and willing to do the small stuff. After calling a half dozen possibilities, I discovered that when contractors advertise, "No job is too small," they often mean they will do the small jobs only in conjunction with a bigger, more profitable project. At last I found a handyman who agreed to do the kind of odd jobs I required. He was scheduled to come the next day, which gave me time to buy some of the new equipment I wanted him to install—a light fixture, two locks, and a spa showerhead.

It wasn't easy walking down the aisles of the local Home Depot. It had been a frequent Sunday morning destination for Steve and me. He was always pointing out the improvements he would make to the house once he'd retired.

The next day, the handyman, Ahmed, arrived at my door. He was courteous and serious, and asked me to show him what I wanted done. I was very pleased

when he said he could start immediately—and immediately finish everything that same day. As he carried
his toolbox into the living room, he stopped before a
picture of Steve and me on my mantelpiece.

Perhaps because he came from a different culture
and was therefore not held back by certain social
restraints, or maybe because he was just curious, he
asked, "Why doesn't your husband do these jobs?
They aren't very complicated. Is your husband a man
who doesn't like to do this kind of work?"

I was quiet for only a moment before I said, "My
husband is gone. He passed several months ago." At
that time, I was still unable to say the word, "died." I
went on, "When my husband was alive, I never had
to call in a professional. He did all the repair jobs on
his own. He was very handy." Somehow it seemed
very important to me to stand up for Steve as a man
who wasn't afraid to get his hands dirty.

Ahmed nodded sympathetically but didn't reply.
Instead, he got on with his work. He installed the
showerhead and the dead bolt, adjusted the dishwasher door, and fixed the leaky faucet. After he
changed the light fixture, he assembled the bookcase without having to read the instructions. He
evidently had the same fix-it gene Steve had had.

I realized that I hadn't even asked him for an
estimate. But he'd done an excellent job. Trusting

him to give me a fair price, I took out my checkbook and asked him to name his fee.

He shook his head and said, "There is no charge. I am only doing what your husband would have done if he were here."

He had been almost silent until then, but after he told me he wasn't charging me for the work he'd done, he became almost voluble.

"My father died when I was a boy. I was too young to help my mother much. But we came from a small village, and the neighbors helped my mother with the chores. It allowed her to spend more time with my sister and me."

He paused briefly and added, "My mother told me never to forget the importance of a small kindness."

He politely refused to stay for tea. Ahmed took his tool box and left, turning once to wave goodbye to me before climbing into his truck. I'd forgotten to ask him to clean the gutters. But he'd managed to help me clear out some of the anger and bitterness that had been in my heart. For, although I would carry the pain of loss with me for the rest of my life, Ahmed reminded me that there was an abundance of good left in the world—and it was now my turn to remember his not-so-small kindness and pay it forward.

—*Marlena Thompson*

Small Change Today,
Philanthropy Tomorrow

When I was young, still in elementary school, I envisioned myself a compassionate philanthropist—although, at the time, I had never heard that word. I just knew that the world needed help, and I stood ready to oblige. Distributing flyers door-to-door for the local Humane Society, pledging a dollar to the Jerry Lewis MDA Telethon, dropping a quarter in the collection box at church—my generosity was boundless.

Not surprisingly, when I grew up I chose to become a social worker. Getting paid to help people seemed too good to be true. I imagined all the important things I would contribute to humankind, elated at the prospect of making myself feel good and making a living at the same time. So I set out to fashion a better world, sacrificing the higher salaries and prestige of other careers to do the important work, the work that needed to be done.

During the course of my career I've worked with troubled adolescents, psychiatric hospital patients, school children, and military families. I've guided people through the confusion of family crises, the despair of unemployment, and every kind of grief and loss imaginable. I like to think of myself as a person who makes a difference.

But enough about me. This isn't a tale of how I've served as an example of benevolence, thereby motivating others to do their part to change the world. It isn't a pat-on-the-back acknowledging my altruism. In fact, as I write this story, my own modest contributions to the world begin to shrink and fade in the shadow of other examples of philanthropy that I never would have imagined as a young child.

This insight came while I was working at a homeless shelter, Samaritan House, where I witnessed all types of giving. There, I saw firsthand the many ways in which people try to make a difference. Many people volunteer their time and donate money, food, clothing, sleeping bags and blankets, personal hygiene products, and other items, hoping to ease the load for others and to give them hope for a better tomorrow. Around the holidays, donations go way up.

Sometimes, the giving is a bit misguided.

There was the woman who called the shelter a couple weeks before Christmas and asked if her children could wrap some of their used toys as gifts for the homeless children, deliver them personally, and watch the kids in the shelter open the presents, so the woman's children could see "how lucky they are" to have the life they have. I explained to her, in gentle terms, that our shelter was not a zoo and that families already at the lowest point in their lives would not appreciate the indignity of being used as a prop to teach others a lesson. I think she felt insulted that we did not appreciate her generosity; she chose to donate nothing at all.

There was the man who called wanting to make a large donation so that he could receive a specific type of tax credit for his own business. When shelter staff could not provide him with detailed technical information about this tax credit, he decried their incompetence and decided to contact a different nonprofit.

A man who volunteered to teach classes at the shelter had a lucrative (for him) idea of how to cash in on the homeless people's plight. He had written a book about the lessons he'd learned working with shelter residents and asked if the agency would market the book for him; in return, he would donate five percent of any profit he made. He didn't understand that, besides the shelter having no staff or money to market his book or anything else, the very idea of his offer was hard to swallow. After all, if he had learned these life-changing lessons from homeless persons, shouldn't they be the ones who profit from it?

Fortunately, such misguided people are the exception rather than the rule. The homeless shelter could not operate without the daily, even hourly, contributions of hundreds of volunteers. Shelter employees who have left to pursue other career opportunities return to work in their former jobs for free. Past residents who now have a space to call home drop off used clothing, books, and kitchen items to repay the kindness shown to them when they needed it most. Retired persons come in three, four, sometimes five days a week to contribute whatever they can, grateful that life has spared them the hardship that others must bear. I have been humbled in the presence of these countless people who give so selflessly—people who, unlike me, give for the sake of giving.

In the midst of all that burgeoning humanity—in the place where I made enough money to pay a mortgage, take vacations, and eat out occasionally—I finally realized what it means to make the world a better place and to inspire others to do the same. It was during our yearly fundraiser—a radio appeal for donations—that I witnessed an event that opened my eyes to the true meaning of philanthropy.

The radio station aired a live broadcast from the shelter parking lot, encouraging listeners to mail in a check or show up during the day to drop off used items for our homeless residents. A dark and windy day yielded to a wet, blustery December evening that kept most people from getting up off their cozy couches and venturing outside. By 9:00 P.M., with only an hour left to go, all of us hard-working employees were cold, tired, and looking forward to being able to go home to our families, warm homes, and TV shows. The economy was in a slump, and the donations were nowhere near the volume we'd received in previous years. All things considered— the lousy weather, the late hour, the low volume of donations—it seemed a bit silly to stick it out until 10:00 o'clock.

Shivering outside in the freezing rain, I saw a man and two kids who looked to be about eight and ten years old ambling across the almost deserted parking lot. *Who on Earth would be walking around with two young kids in the dark on such a night?* The older kid didn't even have a coat on. Despite all the compassion I felt for homeless families, I still sometimes shook my head in frustration. This man should have been looking for shelter before 9:00 on a school night! He should have those kids in a warm, dry place, sleeping softly without a care.

I followed the family inside. It was my job to tell them there was no room for them, not on this night or any night in the foreseeable future. I hoped they had a car; at least that would provide some marginal shelter for them. Soon the schools would be on winter break, and those kids would need a place to stay during the night and the day.

As I entered the homeless shelter, glad for an excuse to come inside, the door greeter pointed me to the conference room, where volunteers were answering the phones to accept pledges. More frustration. *Why had the resident working at the door sent the family there?* Probably because we had a spread of food and hot chocolate for the phone workers; obviously, this family needed it more. I steeled myself for the encounter; I hated turning people away.

When I entered the conference room, I saw the two brothers emptying a few sandwich bags full of change onto the table where our dedicated volunteers attended to the now silent phones. This wasn't a homeless family looking for a place to stay; it was two kids who had pestered their parents to drive them downtown to the shelter, until Dad finally agreed to chauffer them through the slippery streets that accompanied Denver's first winter storm—not even noticing that his older son wasn't wearing a jacket.

One of the phone volunteers, seeing a teachable moment, asked the younger boy if he had saved the money himself. Yes, he said, this was money he had been saving since the first day of school to buy a new Xbox game. She then asked if the brothers knew who they were giving the money to or what is was for. The older boy responded that he had heard on the radio that there were kids who lived here because they had no home of their own. He had heard one kid interviewed on the radio who said that what he wanted for Christmas was either a new power cord or a home.

"We didn't have an extra power cord," he said, "so we thought maybe we could help him get a home."

I doubt either of those kids had ever even heard the word "philanthropist."

—*Sue Dallman-Carrizales*

A Legacy to Carry On

"I guess your work starts now."

The Saturday morning phone call from a neighbor referred to my task as executor of the estate of an old friend, Charlie. During the weekend, I reflected on how I had taken on this job and wondered how I was going to fit it into an already busy schedule. *It shouldn't be too bad,* I reasoned. *They didn't have much, and they were well-organized. It won't take long.*

Charlie and his wife, Pat, were elderly friends of my husband's parents. They had no family in the United States, and all their friends were in their age bracket. Before retirement, Charlie raised some beef in Skamokawa, Washington, on the lower Columbia River, and worked on the Wahkiakum County road crew. In her younger years, Pat did occasional book-keeping, but she viewed her life's work as making a comfortable home for them. Their lives revolved around each other and their cats. They had no children.

Some years previously, Pat had telephoned and asked me to visit one evening. After the usual tea and cookies, the couple asked me to be the executor of their estate.

"We want someone young," they explained, "someone who will outlive us. We have no family here and no close family anywhere. We've left all the instructions with our attorney."

Their anxiety showed on their faces. I knew the attorney and knew we could work together, so I agreed to be their executor. Their relief was immediate. They dragged out their file boxes, proudly showing me how everything was organized. Bank accounts, insurance, bills paid, tax forms, all in neatly labeled manila folders, arranged alphabetically in boxes in a storage closet. They didn't go into detail, just showed me where everything was kept. A neighbor had the key to the house. Upon their deaths, I would have immediate access to their files. I marveled at their efficiency and left relieved that I would be handling the simple estate of a childless, elderly couple who'd worked hard all their lives, lived in a modest home, had nice furniture but few obvious luxuries, traveled occasionally but not extravagantly, and lived quietly.

During my occasional visits over the next several years, I grew to know Pat and Charlie better and discovered we had a number of interests in common. Pat and I shared a passion for a cobalt blue china pattern called "Calico," which we both collected. She had acquired a couple of watercolors that I admired. She and Charlie read avidly, and we occasionally conversed about books. They were well versed in current events and knowledgeable on many topics, and I enjoyed our conversations over tea and cookies.

When Pat became ill with bone cancer and then Alzheimer's disease, she eventually went to live in a local nursing home. I visited her there regularly, although she rarely knew who I was.

After her death, I spent a day with Charlie. I asked if he needed help in settling Pat's estate.

"No, your job will come later," he said. "I can handle this. But do you have any questions?"

I had never seen the will, but as I sat in the living room it occurred to me that I didn't know what was to become of his personal possessions. I ventured the question.

"Don't have any," he said.

"Charlie, I'm sitting here looking at your wedding photo. That's a personal possession."

"Well, I suppose it could go to my nephew. Here, I'll give you his address." His nephew lived in a foreign country.

I pressed on about personal possessions.

He thought for a moment and then said, "You'd better come into the bedroom and look at some things."

He opened the top dresser drawer and began to take out boxes of jewelry. Antique rings, cameos, unusual art deco pieces, fine costume jewelry, and several heavy gold chains filled the boxes. I had never seen any of it before. Shaken at the value it represented, I urged Charlie to put it in a safety deposit box.

"Charlie, if these stones are real, this jewelry is valuable and shouldn't be kept in the house."

"Oh, they're real all right. Pat's family had some money."

"Well, they're truly beautiful, but I'll worry about your safety until I know they're put away."

Charlie made no comment.

Six months after Pat died, Charlie passed on, too. His goal had been to survive her so he could take care of her. When she died, his purpose was fulfilled.

I visited him regularly during those last months, first at his home and then at the assisted-living facility where he moved. I asked several times if he wanted anything done to the house, but he always refused.

"No, Pat decorated it the way she wanted and it pleased me. Of course, I have no taste, but she did. It stays exactly the way she left it."

After Charlie's death, reviewing the will with the lawyer caused the first shock. They had left me a bequest. In fact, they had left me all their personal possessions, including a house full of furniture, photographs, linens, and jewelry. They had never told me.

The second shock occurred when we opened the safety deposit box. I had known about the rings and jewelry, as I had advised Charlie to place them there. I didn't know about the enameled gold and diamond ladies' watch from nineteenth-century Russia. I didn't know about the silver cigarette case or the other Russian silver. I didn't know about the stocks and bonds, the cash, the investments, the multiple bank accounts, or the value of the estate, which eventually reached nearly $700,000. I didn't know they had left their money to nearly a dozen charities representing causes from libraries to environmental preservation. I didn't know that Pat's family had spent time in Russia in the nineteenth century, operating textile mills for a wealthy Russian family.

As I delved into drawers and closets, I discovered notes Pat had left about her possessions: "This cigarette case once was owned by a member of an illustrious Russian family in the days of the Czarist regime . . . He was a member of the Czar's honorary bodyguards . . ." "My grandfather John Boon worked for the Morosov family as mill director and traveled widely in this connection . . . The Morosovs lost everything in the revolution . . ."

Linen towels with Russian motifs, in all probability from one of the Morosov mills, lay folded in a bedroom dresser drawer. I wondered whether a silk scarf commemorating the centenary of the Battle of Borodino, when Napoleon retreated from Russia, was also a product of the mill. A handmade lace frontal for an icon stand, with both English and Russian symbols, spoke of the two worlds Pat's family had lived in. A hand-painted ivory fan from Japan gave evidence of a well-to-do lifestyle in Russia.

"These opera glasses belonged to my grandmother Boon," read a note I found in a desk drawer.

"This antique watch belonged to my grandmother Frances L. G. Boon (nee Settle)—as did my diamond and sapphire ring, diamond and ruby ring, and my diamond band ring," stated a note in the safety deposit box.

Pat had left the notes to help me, but they only hinted at her rich family history. Her files yielded diaries, newspaper clippings, and some genealogical correspondence amplified the notes, as did a published history of the Russian textile industry. Along with a number of other Lancashire families in the 1860s and 1870s, Pat's ancestors had taken up residence in Russia to operate textile mills. They became part of a very small middle class, sharing a quasi-exile from the rest of the country, intermarrying and eventually retiring to England. The story of Pat's family contained all the more poignancy, as I knew no one was left to pass it on to.

I jettisoned the notion that settling the estate would be a simple job. Months of work followed. Gradually, I pulled everything together, cashing in investments and settling accounts and, finally, writing checks to the beneficiaries. Pat and Charlie's possessions enriched several local charities. I felt like Santa Claus to be able to participate in such generosity. And to know that they loved me and left me their treasures, in a way that I could not even thank them, represented such humility of heart.

Several years later, I wear the rings frequently as well as the gold chain with the English gold sovereign with Pat's name and birth date engraved on the reverse. The watch's beauty still shakes me whenever I open its leather case. Pat's Calico coffeepot, one of the scarcer pieces of the pattern, sits on a shelf in my dining room. In my office hangs one of the watercolors, a Northwest beach scene in blues and grays. In my garden, the English daisies, grown from a start from Pat's flower bed, flourish. Occasionally, I receive an annual report from one of the charities to which the couple left a bequest and realize all over again how their legacy furthered this work.

Sometimes, I imagine Pat and Charlie sitting together in the lamplight in their rocking chairs, tea and cookies on the little table between them, chuckling about their estate and the surprises to come. I hope they enjoyed writing their will. I hope they laughed together, picturing my astonishment at the legacy they left me. I hope they gained great pleasure in planning how to do good with the money they'd so diligently earned and carefully managed, though I rather suspect they never quite comprehended the sheer amount of it. I had thought that writing a will must be an onerous and distasteful task. I now know that I shall approach it with joy, in the hope of creating delight and thankfulness and, yes, laughter that will echo long after I am gone.

—*Irene Martin*

Making a Dent

When I was young, I had big plans of growing up and saving the world. But the older I got, the more realistic I became. Injustice, poverty, hunger, and oppression were everywhere. I was but one person. What could I do to alleviate the misery on our planet? Eventually, I realized the best most of us can do is to make a little dent of a difference in some small piece of the world. I found one of those small pieces while looking for stories for an annual report for a university where I was a staff writer.

I was getting a telephone update from the department of ophthalmology. The secretary delivered the usual data: the number of new faculty, research studies underway, and new technology acquired.

"Oh," she added, "and there was a mission trip."

"A mission trip?" I paused. "Tell me about that."

Telling the stories of those who volunteer their time to help others has long been my favorite kind of writing assignment. I wondered how this good news had missed my radar. It turned out I'd missed not one mission, but a couple decades of them. For more than twenty years, the department chairman we often referred to as "Dr. C" had been traveling to remote parts of Mexico several times a year, quietly restoring sight to the blind.

These trips unfolded a bit like a surgical marathon, involving several long days of continuous operations to treat as many patients as possible. When word got out that the eye doctors were coming, hundreds of blind people and their families, often journeying many miles on bare feet, gathered to wait in hopes of treatment. Back when Dr. C first started making the trips, he and his colleague, known simply as "Dr. Tom," hauled equipment on donkeys into remote and sometimes mountainous regions of Southern Mexico. Often, they had no place better to perform eye surgery than the top of a kitchen table.

Most of the surgeries involved removing cataracts, which are the cause of blindness in about half of the 40 to 45 million blind people worldwide. Cataract removal is a relatively simple surgical procedure, but for those in the developing world who lack funds and access to healthcare, it's hard to come by.

It turned out these two surgeons, with the help of various volunteer assistants, had treated more than 12,000 blind people over the years. That struck me as a sizable dent of a difference in a needy part of the world—certainly one worthy of a closer look.

I called the editor of the university magazine and pitched the idea of me volunteering to tag along on the next mission trip and writing a story about it. I got the gig. The next thing I knew, I was taking notes on how to prepare for a mission.

The first thing I learned is that things will, most assuredly, go wrong. The first such event was the tropical storm that hit the day we were hoping to leave, shutting down our mode of transportation—a small, donated airplane complete with a crew. Rather than cancel the mission, Dr. C, a soft-spoken giant of a man, booked us on a commercial flight . . . which evolved into problem number two.

The instruments used in ophthalmologic surgery are too fragile to risk being thrown about in checked baggage and too sharp and dangerous to make it through security as a carry-on. We cast about for ideas, trying to figure out how to get the instruments to the village in time. But then, upon hearing of our mission, the airline staff came to the rescue. They labeled the suitcase containing the instruments with neon stickers marked "Fragile" and assured us the bag would receive extra-special handling. It warmed my heart to see this big commercial airline making its own small dent of a difference to help us out.

But before we even made it through security, problem number three made its appearance, manifested as a look of horror on Dr. C's face.

"I forgot the corneas," he said.

Blindness due to damaged corneas is also a problem in areas lacking healthcare. Donor corneas, provided by an eye bank, are necessary for the transplants. We tried to have faith.

Dr. C called the secretary, who called someone else, who notified a third person, who dropped everything, hopped into a car, retrieved the corneas from a refrigerator, and drove them to another city, where Dr. Tom agreed to intercept them before flying to join us in Mexico. The problem was solved even before we got to the gate. My heart leapt. People were making their little dents of a difference all over the place, and we hadn't even gotten off the ground.

We arrived in Mexico a little after midnight. A young couple in an old van greeted us, grabbed our bags, and chatted happily over the next two hours as we bumped our way over the dark, potholed road and into the city of Huejutla.

After a few hours of sleep in a hot hotel, we threw on scrubs and wandered to a nearby church, where a large crowd had gathered. But they weren't waiting for religious services to begin; they were waiting for us. The crowd grew silent and all eyes were upon us. "*Buenos dias!*" we said many times, as we eased our way through the mass of patients waiting to be seen.

I brought along a camera, a notebook, and a tape recorder, but before I knew it, my writing tools were stashed under a table and I was setting up an operating room in a church hall. Though I had worked for about eight years as a registered nurse many years before, nothing in my training or clinical experience had prepared me for this.

The first order of the day was tracking down a soldering iron to fix one of the surgical microscopes. It had been damaged on a recent "field trip" to the mountains to treat the blind who lived too far afield to travel to a mission site. Before long, the microscope was repaired and we were ready for patients.

Most of the patients already screened had severe cataracts. In the United States, cataracts are normally removed when the eye's lens becomes cloudy; it is then replaced with an intraocular lens. In these patients without access to healthcare, the lenses had become the color of iced tea, rendering them blind. With so many people needing surgery, we were able to treat only one eye per patient.

As patients came and went, gently guided by a few volunteers, I noted an extraordinary aura of patience and calm, despite the profound and abundant need for treatment. The area designated for pre-op preparation was stifling in the heat, but it was so quiet it was almost prayerful.

A similar atmosphere prevailed in the holding area for those waiting to have surgery. Without the typical calming pre-op drugs, the patients lying side by side on simple cots quietly told stories to pass the time. One man reflected on a childhood memory of the Mexican Revolution. Another recalled the events that took place the year he lost his vision.

After I'd observed a few cases, Dr. C said it was time for me to assist. Once I got the hang of things, we developed a streamlined system: while I cleaned and set up a new tray of instruments, Dr. C would treat a patient with another assistant. While she cleaned and set up a new tray, he would treat the next patient with me assisting. Soon, we were operating at an admirable pace.

Evening came, and the delicious smells of people cooking black beans and tortillas outside diluted the scent of the alcohol we used to sterilize instruments. Someone began to play a guitar, and soon there was singing. Though we were exhausted, the energizing music kept us going a few more hours.

The next two days were much like the first, except that Dr. Tom, who had flown in with the corneas, joined us with his team of assistants. With a steady stream of patients coming and going, it seemed like we were actually getting somewhere.

My belief was reinforced when I tagged along with Dr. C to check patients who'd had surgery the day before. He pulled the patch from the eye of one young man who had been blind in both eyes. When his treated eye opened, the man immediately gave way to an enormous smile and said, "No sabia que las cosas se veian asi." ("I didn't know things looked like that.")

In the course of three days, we treated 163 people, most of whom were blind and went away seeing. It was a pretty good dent, and I felt privileged to have helped make it.

As we walked out the door to head to the airport, a crowd of people reached out to shake our hands. I will never forget the look of gratitude and hope on their faces. It was difficult to leave, but I knew the team would return.

I have since gone on two more "vision" missions to Mexico. Though we can't fix all of the problems in the world or even in Mexico, at least we're making a dent of a difference in this small piece of the world.

—Susan Sarver

The Benevolence of Mindfulness

There are two ways to get into Albuquerque from the Sandia Mountains in New Mexico, where I grew up. There is the big four-lane interstate, "I-40," and the meandering two-lane road known as "Old 66." My mom always chooses the old road.

"I have to look at things," she says.

On numerous drives throughout my life, she would suddenly pull over to examine a weed flowering by the side of the road or rescue a beetle from certain tragedy on the blacktop, while I, in my late teens and early twenties, sat impatiently in the car. I just wanted to get to wherever I was going.

Though Mother's Day follows Earth Day, for me, they have always been related. My mom has been "green" since before concern about the environment was given a trendy color code. Part of this impulse was born of thrift. Like her mother and her grandmother before that, Mom saves glass jars and empty cottage cheese containers, and she washes and reuses her plastic storage bags. She buys many of her clothes second-hand, and when a button falls off or a seam comes apart, she mends her clothes instead of replacing them. Her hall closet is crammed with paper bags and boxes awaiting a new purpose.

One such box, known as "the girdle box," which bore a pink and gray line drawing of a woman in her foundation garments, was exchanged by our extended family at holidays for over fifteen years. One year the box traveled from Mom's hometown of Rapid City, South Dakota, to relatives in Burney, California, then on to Albuquerque the next year. After a time, the box was so celebrated that receiving it almost trumped the value of what was inside.

Mom never set out to save the planet, but the way she cultivates her own environment is a lesson to those recent converts to the "green" life. Mom's daily summer ritual of breakfast (yogurt, granola, and fruit) taken at the little metal table outside her back door affords her the chance to check up on her yard. Because she is mindful, she identifies the little green seedling poking through the stones in her patio as a "volunteer" from last summer's cosmos. She attends the opening of a flower or the arrival of the hummingbirds with the same awe others might reserve for an opera or the first baseball game of the season.

"I put a little dish of water out for the butterflies," she said to me one day, her voice vibrating with delight, "and yesterday there were three swallowtails."

She goes on to regale me with tales of the snake who swallowed three of her fish and the coyote who stood outside her bedroom window and just stared at her.

"They're tricksters," she says. "I think he wanted me to laugh."

Mom creates a kind of give-and-take relationship with wildlife in her yard. She knows to pick the apples on her trees a little early to fend off the bears and that, if she leaves the bird feeders out at night, it's likely they'll be knocked down by a family of raccoons. Spiders that make their way into the house are captured in a juice glass and set loose in the garden.

"My juncos are back," she says. "They're fighting the squirrels for the seed in the feeder. Those little buggers seem to give everyone a run for their money."

After living in Los Angeles for nearly fifteen years, I like hearing these stories of Mom's own personal wilderness. Now that I am older and my two small children have set time to running, like a flooded arroyo, I am grateful for Mom's measured pace. When I visit her and we drive together, I share her wonder as the setting sun tips the clouds toward tangerine. In the mountains of New Mexico, we search together for the delicate Mariposa lily. On her California visits, we head to a local public garden or sit quietly in the vast urban wilderness of Griffith Park. Her gentle presence reminds me to keep my ears and eyes open. In this way, I might hear water dropping from a leaf or see a brown lizard creep a little farther into the sun.

"I got eight-tenths of an inch of rain last night," Mom tells me. "And this morning it was only thirty degrees. Tonight, I bet we'll get snow."

At sixty-three, her voice holds the same amount of glee as my five-year-old son's when he contemplates a winter wonderland. "Snow," she says. "I love the smell of snow."

I am slowing down, and it isn't because of the weight of my nearly forty years on the planet; it is out of my concern for the planet itself. I've begun to save glass jars and re-use packing envelopes. I pause in my daily tasks to watch the squirrels race each other through the palm leaves above my porch.

I try to teach my children that looking out for the environment starts with being aware of the environment. On busy streets, we look for spent dandelions to parachute, we say hello to neighborhood cats, and we pick up the plastic cups and paper bags cluttering the gutters. This teaching comes easily, I realize, because I was taught so well by example. Mom didn't need to lecture; she didn't need to beat a drum to change the world. She simply slowed down enough to enjoy living in it and with that joy came compassion and an instinct for preservation.

Last summer, in the company of my son and daughter, I planted tomatoes in my yard. With the heat of August around me like a mantle, I ate the first fruit while sitting on my low wall with dirt on my hands. Warm from the sun, it burst on my tongue with a sweetness I immediately wanted to share with my mom.

—*Tanya Ward Goodman*

A version of this story first appeared in the online literary journal Literary Mama, *under the title "Mom Takes the Slow Road."*

Generosity Knows No Stranger

Surrounded by a lobby full of agitated travelers, I had never felt so alone. My husband had died a few months earlier, and old friends had suggested I meet them in Alabama for a winter break. It seemed like a good idea; it was time I began traveling by myself in this new period in my life. But now I was stranded in Dallas by an unexpected spring snowstorm.

Before we landed, the airline had given us a phone number to call to rebook flights and to make hotel reservations. I had done both. Although the transmission broke up before I received my motel confirmation, I'd been told I had a room and they had my credit card number. There would be a shuttle, and an airport employee told me where to stand outside—in the snowy rain—to be picked up. However, no shuttles arrived from anywhere. Apparently, the snow and slush had paralyzed traffic.

After nearly two hours, I managed to squeeze into a crowded taxicab, which dropped me off at the motel. A long line of travelers stood at the desk in front of an obviously frustrated young man, who kept repeating that the motel was full. By the time I arrived at the desk, the clerk was barely able to remain civil. They hadn't had a room available since noon, he said, and he had no idea why they were so overbooked. No names had been put on the waiting list since early afternoon, and there was no record of my reservation. The desk clerk said I could call the airline and see what had caused the problem, but they simply had no available rooms. When asked if there were any other accommodations in the area, he said the closest available motel room was eighty miles away.

"But what can I do?" I asked. "I have a flight out at six-thirty in the morning."

"When the shuttle returns, we'll send you back to the airport. You can spend the night there."

He beckoned for the next person to come up to the desk.

Now what? I didn't want to spend the night in the airport. I didn't know whether the airport had any secure or private areas where I would feel comfortable sleeping. Staying in the motel lobby seemed safer.

I found an empty wing chair in a corner in the lobby and realized that by turning it slightly I couldn't be seen from the desk. I settled down into my hiding place and began a silent conversation with my husband. Even though he was no longer with me, these "talks" were always comforting. I felt he was still looking after me and giving answers whenever I felt overwhelmed by my new life. No answers came—only the urge to visit the ladies' room. I tried desperately to ignore the inevitable. I finally gave in, crept out of my chair, and found the restroom. It was locked—the last straw. I felt like an abandoned child. *Stiff upper lip*, I told myself as I leaned against the wall, shut my teary eyes, and waited for the occupant to leave.

In spite of my efforts to hold it in, my misery must have been obvious. A gentle voice asked if I were all right. Opening my eyes, I saw the voice belonged to a kindly hotel maid. Her compassion induced a flood of tears, and I sobbed out my story, only to realize how slight my problem sounded. Suddenly, the ladies' room door opened and I fled inside, embarrassed about breaking down in front of a stranger. I did my business, told myself that it would be okay no matter what, washed my face, and tried to look composed.

Much to my surprise, the maid was waiting for me outside the restroom. "I talked to the clerk," she said. "There's no room here, but he is dialing a hotel service agency, and you can talk to them directly. Just go to the desk; he'll put you on the phone."

I thanked her and went back into the lobby. The desk clerk greeted me and told me to wait just a few minutes; the phone was busy but he'd dial it for me once it was free. The crowd had thinned out. A female clerk was also now at the desk, maybe giving her male counterpart time to be more cordial. The new clerk was deep into a discussion with a slender woman about the location of the stairs.

Who cares? I thought absently. *Must be one of those people who climb stairs for exercise.*

Then I was handed the phone and began talking to another distant voice.

The female clerk interrupted my call. "Are you traveling alone?" she asked.

"Of course." *Didn't she know my problem? Why else would I be using the desk clerk's phone?*

"This guest would like to share her suite with you," the clerk continued. "She asked me if I knew a single woman who needed a place to stay."

I looked up in amazement at the woman beside me, the one who'd been asking about the stairs.

"I felt so selfish when I realized I had a whole suite to myself when so many people need rooms," she said. "So I asked the clerk to find someone to share with. There's a sofa that makes up into a bed if you would like to have it."

Share a room with a stranger? I'd heard many warnings about strangers over the years, but hadn't I prayed for a room? Here was my answer. What could I do but accept?

It turned out to be an unbelievably wonderful experience. We discovered we had much in common. We were both readers who didn't watch television; her children and my grandchildren shared a passion for the American Girl dolls; and we were leaving for the airport at the same time the next morning.

I bought breakfast. We shared the shuttle, and then separated to catch our respective planes. Mine left on time, and I had a marvelous—and uneventful—holiday on the Gulf Coast.

Since then, I've told this story to many of my friends. Their reaction is usually, "I don't think I would be willing to share my room with a stranger."

I wouldn't have, either—at least not before a perfect stranger answered my prayer and gave me shelter that lonely, stormy night. Since then, though, when I see a stranger in need, instead of telling myself it's none of my business, I ask myself, "How can I help?"

—*Sybilla A. Cook*

The Face Beneath the Hood

When I walked into the women's shelter that sweltering Sunday night, a slim woman was already there, huddled in the corner. I could barely make out her face, as she had hid it with the hood of her sweatshirt. I tried to say hello but she refused to make eye contact and shifted away from me. Most of the women I've met at the shelter have been friendly and warm, but once in a while I run into one who is so beaten down, she can barely function. Some are mentally ill. But this time I felt fear. My immediate thought was to keep a close watch on Levi, my nine-year-old son, and to wear my pocketbook across my chest.

On the second Sunday of every month, my temple serves dinner at a local women's shelter. The women are given meals during the week, but on weekends they are left to fend for themselves. The area's temples and churches all pitch in to cover those nights when the residents otherwise might go hungry. I signed up my family because I wanted to help others and also because I wanted my son to get in the habit of helping others at an early age.

Sometimes Levi helped make the meal. Sometimes he helped set up. Sometimes, while my husband and I served, he would just watch—and learn. Learn that not everyone enjoys his good fortune. Learn that those who are different or down on their luck are still people who could joke and talk with him, who are still worthy of respect. I wanted him to move past fear and pity and to see the person . . . which is what I was failing to do miserably on that hot night.

It had to be ninety degrees in the shelter's dining room, and yet the woman was bundled up, glowering out from her hood. I couldn't see so much as feel two fierce eyes, daring me to mess with her. I nervously avoided her as I went about my business of setting up, praying that some of the other volunteers would show up soon.

As if on cue, Alice, another temple member, arrived. No-nonsense Alice looked around and sized up the situation in an instant. Without pause, she loaded up a plate of food, marched over to the woman, and began talking. At first, Alice received only grunts in response. Then, the woman slowly raised her head and pulled back the hood. I almost dropped a plate from the shock. This was no tough woman, but a girl, maybe sixteen or eighteen. As Alice engaged her, the girl slowly dropped her pose, began to smile and become animated. She shyly accepted the food.

Later, I asked Alice what they talked about, and Alice related that the girl did have a job but it was minimum wage. She got behind in her rent and lost her apartment.

"Doesn't she have family who can help?" I asked.

Alice smiled ruefully, "She said, 'I only have my mother, and she doesn't care what happens to me.'"

Hot shame raced over me. This was a scared, confused kid trying to find her place in the world, probably kicked so many times that her only defense was to hide behind that hood. I felt admiration for her having the tenacity and courage to still mount a pose to ward off potential threats.

I never saw the girl again after that. I pray that's because she got back on her feet. But I think of her often and silently thank her and Alice. I learned a lot from them that night, things I should have already known about appearances and judging. This child was nothing to be afraid of; her initial tough stance was her guard against her own fear. As a writer, I should have known that everyone, no matter how scary looking, has a story to tell.

Now that this girl has torn my blinders off, I see the women in the shelter now, really see them. I not only serve them food, I also talk and listen. There is the woman whose last job was in the World Trade Center. When it was destroyed, along with her employer's business, her tightly woven world came unraveled. She stays at the shelter because it also offers job training.

"I will do what it takes to get back on my feet," she says with determination and not a lick of self-pity.

Then there is the woman who looks like your basic suburban mom. I had assumed she was an employee at the shelter and was surprised to learn she is a resident. Turns out she is on the run from an abusive husband. When breaking bread together with these women, we each cast off our metaphorical hood and see each other's faces and inside each other's souls. It's a start.

I came to volunteer in the shelter because I wanted to help and I wanted my son to learn. The bonus is how much I learn as well. How wide is the world when we choose to let it in. How rich is life when we recognize that we are all in it together.

—Beth Levine

Trash Talk

Faster than a whirling tornado, five gray garbage cans roll down the cul-de-sac, rumbling as they make their escape from my neighbor's front curb.

"Quick, grab that lid," I instruct my six-year-old daughter.

I dash after the blowing bins, determined to corral them to their proper location.

"I got one, Mama," my daughter grins, sprinting my way with a blue Rubbermaid® lid. "But why are you getting those cans? Don't they belong to those funny people who never talk to us?"

I stop in my tracks, right in front of my neighbor's spacious Tudor. The three-car garage, home to a sleek black Mercedes and red Porsche convertible, seems to sneer at the basic Chevy sedan parked in my driveway. Though they are just across the street, their life seems far removed from my reality. Every week, I peer out my dining room window, envy creeping forward with every housecleaner, doggy groomer, and landscaper that pulls up their driveway.

"Their boys must go to the academy," I remarked one day to my husband, raising my eyebrows as two boys walked out of the house clad in clothing that screamed "exclusive private school": crisply pressed khaki pants and blue sport coats emblazoned with diamond-shaped crests.

Perhaps my face, green with envy, has kept my neighbors from crossing the street and introducing themselves. Though we have lived in the neighborhood for three years, jealously has stolen my usual outgoing nature, keeping me from outstretching my hand in greeting.

"Those people don't even answer the door," my ten-year-old complained, coming home empty-handed from a Girl Scout cookie sales call.

"Maybe they aren't home," I rationalized, trying to hide the crack in my voice. (I secretly wondered if my neighbors were "above" eating Trefoils or Thin Mints.)

"Yeah, right," my daughter replied, rolling her eyes. "I could hear their TV blaring."

Sarcasm has a way of bouncing from mother to daughter, like a nasty case of stomach flu. I grimaced, badly wanting to reverse my fourth grader's jaded world view. Here I was, judging a family I didn't even know.

Maybe they weren't even happy with their material possessions. Maybe they longed for the "things" that filled our home: laughter, love, and family.

Today, I feel the warm winds of change blowing right down the cul-de-sac. I chase this second chance, grabbing hold of a tumbling trash pail and sitting it upright.

"It's just the right thing to do," I tell my six-year-old as I stop to catch my breath. "If our cans were blowing down the street, I bet they'd do the same thing for us."

My kindergartener's eyes sparkle, her eyebrows not yet furrowed with her older sister's doubt. "They'd help us, too," she repeats, skipping off to gather the fifth and final lid.

Although I am tempted to test this theory by "accidentally" pushing our cans down the street, I refrain.

The next morning at the bus stop, I wave and smile as a familiar red Porsche revs its engine and pulls out of the cul-de-sac. In return, I receive a friendly head nod.

"Wave 'good morning,'" I instruct my daughters.

But they are more concerned with the wiggly worms on the sidewalk than my outreach efforts.

"Where's the bus?" they ask, ignoring my request.

"It's running late," I answer . . . just like my attempt to teach basic human kindness. Why should I now expect a simple wave or retrieved garbage can to make an impact?

That afternoon, I volunteer to read *Frog and Toad* to my daughter's kindergarten reading group. The story of two unlikely friends' foibles—Frog trying to help Toad secure a melting ice cream cone on a sultry summer day—makes me laugh. I now wonder if the author was trying to send me a message about unselfish giving.

"Thanks for helping today," the teacher says as I collect the books from the children.

"Sure," I answer, pausing in the hallway to admire a collage of colorful crayon drawings.

"You have to see this one." The teacher points to a picture of two black bins lying on their side like road kill. "That was really great how you helped your neighbors."

"She told you about that?" I ask, trying hard to read my daughter's "invented" spelling and down-hill uppercase printing: "WE RAN AFTR THE CANS."

"Yeah, I had a neighbor like that once," the teacher winks. "He never talked to me, either."

Long after the classroom door closes, I linger, admiring the drawing of two smudgy-black bins tipped on their sides in the middle of a charcoal gray street. Though empty, their message of kindness and basic respect overflows, softening my heart.

In the afternoon, I stand at the bus stop, smiling and waving at passersby like a princess in a parade. Although I don't have throngs of neighborly admirers (my waves are lost in a cloud of Porsche exhaust fumes), I know two little girls are watching my every move. *Be positive*, I tell myself. *Never stop reaching out.*

"I'll watch your son after school," I say to the lady who lives next door.

Making sure my daughters are within earshot, I greet a new couple down the street. "I'd be happy to drive your kids to choir," I smile.

On our refrigerator, a crayon drawing of two garbage pails reminds me that even the smallest steps can leave indelible imprints. "WE RAN AFTR THE CANS," I read for the hundredth time. Now, that's trash talk even a mother can be proud of.

—*Stefanie Wass*

This story was first published in the Christian Science Monitor, *July 2, 2009.*

The Power of Pebbles

I once heard that the smallest pebble tossed into a river can cause a slight shift in the water's flow. And when that pebble is joined by millions of other pebbles, it can change the river's course forever. Here's what I know of pebbles. . .

Since the time doctors diagnosed my daughter, Kiki, with a rare form of dwarfism called Kniest syndrome, we've watched and waited for things to happen. We watched and waited for when her back might curve to a debilitating point, for when her hips might grow such that they would interfere with her ability to walk, or for when one of her retinas might detach, requiring immediate surgery to avoid permanent blindness.

By age eight and on the cusp of starting third grade, Kiki's lower legs had splayed to a point that walking had become labored. When she stood, her knees met but her lower legs grew out to the side to a severe degree. Her orthopedic surgeon recommended surgery that would straighten her lower limbs.

For all our worrying, though, we'd been fortunate so far in that Kiki had avoided surgeries for as long as she did. Others we knew with Kniest had undergone several operations by the time they were Kiki's age. Still, the brutally invasive procedure meant Kiki would spend six weeks in a pair of thigh-high casts and then as many weeks, if not more, relearning to walk.

I'd hoped to schedule the surgery early in the summer, giving Kiki time to recuperate before going back to school. Plans are one thing, reality another. The earliest available date for surgery was the first week in August. That still gave her a few weeks to recover before the start of school, but it meant she'd enter third grade in her casts and wheelchair.

With all of the physical challenges Kiki faced, I worried, too, about how her peers would react to her differences. I suppose this concern looms in the periphery of most parents of children with special needs, especially for parents of children who are cognitively aware of their physical limitations. I held my breath, waiting for the day Kiki would come home from school saying someone had called her a name or teased her for being small or for walking a bit differently. I half expected the teasing to come sooner rather than later. Many parents I knew talked about how cruel kids can be and how their children had faced intolerance. Though Kiki had been spared such cruelty from her peers thus far, I worried how they would respond now. Would she be made fun of or left out?

Because I work full-time, my mother flew to Michigan from her home in Arizona to assist Kiki while she was at school. She sat with Kiki through all of her classes and reported back to me on all of the happenings. She said Kiki got right back into the thick of school and into hanging out with her friends, and that her friends took turns pushing her in her wheelchair from classroom to classroom. Kiki came home each day with new signatures on her casts from classmates and teachers.

After Kiki's hard casts came off, she spent another several weeks in removable soft casts. Not long after that, the work began. With close to two months of no walking, Kiki had lost a lot of strength in her legs. She'd never experienced anything as painful and intrusive before, and the surgery had chipped away some of her spunk. She needed help not only in building physical strength but also in building confidence in her ability to stand and then to walk again. Every morning before school, a couple of times after school, and periodically throughout the weekend, we would help and encourage Kiki to stand. During the school day, my mother would wheel Kiki out of the classroom a few times each day so she could practice standing. To help boost Kiki's confidence, I also arranged to come to school during her lunch hour when she began working on standing and getting used to putting weight on her legs again. The first day, I checked in at the office. I walked down the long empty hallway and found my mom and Kiki waiting just outside the classroom. Kiki's classmates were outside for lunchtime recess. Kiki smiled as she always does when she sees me unexpectedly, and she stretched her arms out to embrace me in a hug. I kissed her on the cheek, and we got to work.

I grasped Kiki's hands and my mother held her from behind, under her arms. We encouraged her to stand for a few minutes and then rest and then stand again. She met the task with grace and bravery, her tiny body shaking while she struggled to maintain balance. During the second week of my lunch-time visits, I arrived a bit late one day because of a work assignment. I checked in at the office as usual, and then met my mom and Kiki, who were again waiting in the hallway. Kiki pushed herself to a standing position as her classmates began filtering in from recess. They milled about the hallway, getting water and stopping at the bathroom, as my mom held Kiki under the arms and I took her hands again, this time to walk a few steps. As she cautiously took small steps, one by one her classmates shouted encouragements as they made their way into the classroom.

"Way to go, Kiki!" I heard one of her classmates say.

"Yeah, Kiki! You're walking," another said.

I struggled to maintain my composure and concentrate on the task at hand, as I couldn't quite grasp what I was hearing. I'd focused for so long on preparing Kiki and myself for how cruel kids could be that I was unprepared for how compassionate they actually were.

I realize the cruelty that others have described experiencing comes from a current of intolerance that has run in the same direction for a long time, but Kiki's classmates, my pebbles, are changing that current. It may be a small change, a subtle shift, but it is a shift all the same. These children haven't just learned compassion for a fellow classmate. I believe they live and breathe it. They will remember it when they have their own children, and the current will continue to shift, until perhaps one day it will change forever.

—*Cristina Trapani-Scott*

Child by Child

One cool autumn day in 1957, when I was eight years old, I sat on the front stoop with my black lab, Penny. My duck, Donald, pecked in the grass nearby. Penny spent my childhood with me, and I'd won Donald at a fair. Donald and Penny, my duck-hunting dog, were the best of friends.

Earlier that day a new family started moving in just two doors down from our house. Their truck was overflowing with furniture, toys, and other household odds and ends. I watched two men unload the moving van and hand off smaller items to a woman in the doorway. After a little while, Penny and I headed up the street on a walk.

As we passed the house with the truck parked in front, I stopped because something caught my eye: a wheelchair stood in the middle of the grass in the front yard. I watched, curious to see what might come off the truck next. The woman came out and pushed the chair toward the house, pausing for a moment to look at us and smile. I wondered what she thought about a girl, a dog, and a duck taking a walk together.

Penny, Donald, and I circled the block and then I sat back down on the stoop. I looked up the street and saw that the truck was empty. Just then, a car pulled up, and one of the men opened the door of the car, reached in, and scooped up a young boy. He looked to be about my age. The man carried him into the house. I thought the boy must not be able to walk and that maybe the wheelchair was for him.

The next day was a Monday. After school, I walked by the house where the new family now lived. I wanted to meet the new boy, so I knocked on the door.

The woman who answered said, "Hi, can I help you?"

"Yes, I live down the street, and I noticed you have a boy who might be my age. Could I meet him?"

"Sure," she said and invited me in. She introduced me to her son, Johnny, who sat in the wheelchair.

"Hi, Johnny, do you want to play?"

"Sure."

His mom pushed the chair toward his bedroom, and I followed. The room was full of boxes, but the bed was set up and there was a box of toys on the floor. A round braided rug covered most of the floor. Johnny climbed out of the chair and got down on the floor. His left hand jerked, and he dragged his left leg. His brown hair framed a bright smile. He eagerly suggested games and things we could do. I felt awkward at first, but as we played, we laughed together and the awkwardness fell away. The box was full of miniature toys, animals, barns, houses, tractors, and people. So we set up a farm and played for a long time.

I asked him why he hadn't gone to school today.

"They don't let kids like me go to school," he said.

"What?" I said. "Why not?"

His mom heard our conversation and came into the room. She explained that Johnny had cerebral palsy and they didn't have a place for kids with disabilities in the public schools. I knew that was unfair and decided I should do something about it, so I offered to come by each day after school and read and write with Johnny. His mom thought this was an excellent idea. She agreed that I could bring my dog and duck when the weather was nice and we could be outside.

The next day I stopped by after school with Donald and Penny trailing. Johnny sat in his wheelchair in the backyard while his mom hung up wet laundry.

Johnny laughed and clapped his hands when he saw Donald and Penny. Penny cozied up next to the wheelchair, and Johnny petted her. I picked up Donald and put him in Johnny's lap. He'd never stroked a duck before, and he liked it. Donald quacked and pecked at his fingers. Johnny thought that to be very funny.

Leaning against the trunk of a huge walnut tree that spread across a large portion of the backyard, I watched and thought, *Johnny seems so happy. He knows how to appreciate things.*

His mom asked, "Do you want some lemonade and cookies?"

"Sure," we said.

So we went inside and sat at the table.

"Here, look, I brought some math papers home— and my reading book." I took them out of a bag and laid them on the table.

Johnny looked excited.

So we ate cookies, drank lemonade, and looked at the math papers together. We laughed when crumbs covered some of the numbers. Johnny's parents had already taught him many of the numbers, so we worked on adding and subtracting. Then we looked at my reader. He knew his alphabet and a little about sounding out words. We spent the rest of the afternoon taking turns reading out loud. When he stumbled over a word, I helped him.

I went to Johnny's house every day after school for months. I taught him everything as I learned it, and he became an excellent reader and was also very good at math. I'd make up quizzes for him to take, and I'd give him spelling tests I'd taken in class.

After the school year came to an end, I continued going to Johnny's house. I tried to every day, and I often brought Penny and Donald with me. Johnny loved Penny, and she would sit next to him while we worked or played on the floor. I knew she made Johnny happy because he would laugh and laugh when I brought her along. Donald and Penny together, well, that made us both laugh. Sometimes Penny would lay there, and Donald would snuggle in along her stomach. Then she would push her head slightly under a wing and close her eyes.

I was sure Johnny belonged in school, and I had a hard time understanding why there wasn't a place for him.

As I grew up, I found out there were many injustices in the public school system. Later that summer, Johnny told me he had to move again. One day, I walked past the house on my way home from school. There was Johnny sitting in his chair watching his dad and a couple of guys load stuff on a truck. His shoulders were hunched, and he looked so alone. Penny and Donald were with me. We stopped and sat on the grass next to Johnny. For a while, neither of us said anything.

Then I said, "I'm really going to miss you, Johnny."

"I'm going to miss you too. You're the only friend I've ever had." Tears welled up in his eyes.

I touched his hand. I felt his sadness, and my heart felt heavy. I thought, *His only friend? How could that be? He is one of the sweetest people I know.* I wondered why someone wouldn't want to be his friend.

It turned out that his new house was just a couple of blocks from the school I went to. So I told Johnny I'd visit him at his new house after school, too. Johnny looked forward to seeing me again, and this made the move more bearable. Our relationship continued until I moved to Colorado after fourth grade.

I learned so much from my experiences with Johnny, and I became very comfortable with people who were different than me. As I grew up, my relationship with Johnny influenced how I treated people who were different. Thinking about the injustices in our world, I decided to work with children. I felt strongly that children with special needs belonged in school, and I was pleased when on November 29, 1975, Public Law 94-142 was signed into law. Implemented in October 1977, the Individuals with Disabilities Education Act, as it is now called, protected the rights of individuals with special needs and also assured that they would have access to education. It was during this time that I started studying special education in college.

After graduating, I went on to work with children who were emotionally disturbed, who had learning disabilities, autism, and physical challenges. Each child was so unique, and I learned as much from them as they did from me. I touched their lives, and they touched mine. Almost every child I worked with met the world with eagerness and hope. They also met each challenge with a willingness to try. I can only hope that I made a difference in their lives, that somehow I made their reality a little more bearable, satisfying, and joyful.

When I reflect on those years now, I see that that is how we each can make a difference in the world—child by child, person by person, like making a beaded necklace. Each bead is put on the string, one by one, until the circle is complete. Each bead touches another and is touched by another until all are connected.

—Linda Stork

Heroes on Harleys

When I was a kid growing up in Western Oregon, timber country, summer vacation meant exploring the woods and lounging around our out-in-the-boonies home. After a few weeks, though, we were all ready for some excitement.

The summer I was ten, excitement came like a wave of thunder roaring up our long, steep gravel driveway. The surrounding fir trees camouflaged the source of the sound. It started with a rumble just loud enough to break up the country quiet and then grew to a pulsing growl that no kid could ignore. Matt, Jennifer, and I rushed to the high deck on the front of our house. We watched with both fascination and fear as, one after another, a gang of motorcycle-riding, tattoo-displaying, long-haired bikers came riding up to the house.

My stepmom, Joanne, ushered us quickly inside and warned the three of us to stay put. She went out through the basement to meet with our rough-looking visitors. Jennifer, older than me by a year and always the protector, scooted our little brother, Matt, and me toward the closet door, ready to push us in for safety.

Moments ticked by, and I wondered what had happened to my stepmom. *Was she okay? Were they going to take her?* Eyeing the .22 rifle leaned up against the closet wall, I imagined all sorts of horrific scenarios. Fear began to take its toll on me. My hands shook and I felt like crying, but more than that, I didn't want Jennifer to be disappointed in my baby-like behavior, so I held on. Matt wanted to peek out the window. At only four, he was little, lively, and had a habit of bursting into giggles. *How, I wondered, could we keep him quiet if we had to hide in the closet?*

When I thought I couldn't stand it another minute, the unthinkable happened. The sound stilled our nervous feet. Familiar and reassuring, the high-pitched clucking laughter of my stepmom floated like a safety rope through the open window. Jennifer and I often used this unusual beacon to find her in crowded grocery stores or rooms of socializing adults.

My shoulders softened, and my fears were replaced by curiosity.

We gathered in a pile at the living room window and gazed down at our driveway. Every square inch had been filled by motorcycles, some tipped up in the front with long reaching handlebars, others sparkling with shiny chrome. A group of men and a few women had gathered and were laughing along with my stepmom. A wave of her hand gave us the okay, and we raced downstairs and outside. I darted toward my stepmom and stood close by her side. Matt kept his body behind her legs, his arms wrapped around them. When he thought no one was looking, he'd tip his head and sneak a peek at the crowd.

One man appeared to lead the group. He stood before us, his heavy-set body clad in leather and decorated with tattoos. Something about him seemed familiar. When he spoke, I recognized the playful growly voice. Fritz, as they called him, worked alongside my dad at one of the local mills. I'd never seen him in his biker regalia before, but his full smile and belly laugh set me totally at ease.

With a signal from Fritz, everyone stilled and quieted. He reached into his shirt pocket and pulled out a small piece of paper. Handing it to my stepmom, he explained that the group had wanted to help with Matt's medical expenses. With a quick flash of emotion and a bright smile that creased her eyes, Joanne quietly and graciously accepted the gift—a sizeable check.

Before that day, I'd never given any thought to the expenses that my brother's illness incurred. Somehow, our parents protected us from the realities of a desperate situation. Matt had been diagnosed with a genetic disorder, Gaucher's disease, when he was just a baby. His body, unable to make a particular enzyme, fought against itself. The disease was so rare that much of his testing and treatment took place on the East Coast, a long way from our home. As a mother, now, of my own four children, I still can't imagine what it must have been like for my parents. Each day, the bills must have mounted, and yet no cure appeared.

The lazy comfort of my childhood nirvana was momentarily replaced by the knowledge that this money was greatly needed and should not be turned down out of pride. My new reality was one of community. These men and women had put together a large sum of money because they cared. They were more concerned with bringing comfort and security to another than to indulging in extras for themselves.

Times were tough in our little community. Mills were closing, and the timber industry was in the midst of a fall from greatness to destitution. My dad would watch the news each night to see the list of mills that would or would not be running the next day. Everyone was impacted, but that didn't stop the community from rallying around our family.

When Matt needed a bone marrow transplant, the parking lot of our grocery store became a clinic, and people flooded in to be tested. Prisoners organized a run to benefit Matt at the penitentiary. Softball games and dances were held, and the money raised at those events went right into Matt's medical account. And when, at nearly eight years old, Matt passed away, our community overfilled the church and spread out into the parking lot to say goodbye. After all, Matt had become family to them, too.

I still miss my brother, and this past January we had to say goodbye to my stepmom. Only Dad, Jennifer, and I are left, but we still have this community that embraced us in our times of grief as well as in our times of celebration.

It's been more than twenty-five years since those motorcycles came barreling up our driveway, bringing desperately needed money—and more. Their generosity that day showed my family that other people cared, and it changed something within me. It taught me that people should be judged by what they do, not by how they look, and that blessing others can bring joy to both the recipients and the givers. Fritz didn't need to have the check tugged from his hand. His biker cronies did not need to be strong-armed to contribute their dollars. They gave freely and gladly. The smiles that spread across their faces as Fritz handed over the check to Joanne spoke of their compassion and their love. So, when you see a group of rough-riding bikers, don't just turn away in fear. Because inside those leather jackets may beat the hearts of angels.

—*Christina Suzann Nelson*

Quit Talkin' and Start Doin'

"For almost ten years, we've been discussin' our personal problems and the problems in this fast-growing community," our Texas leader drawled. "It's time we quit talkin' and start doin'!"

"Are you serious, Mary?" Barbara asked the leader of our small Bible study group. "The other night I had a dream of a care center. People were streaming in from all over the county looking for help," she added, eyes sparkling with excitement.

"A care center, huh? Well, I've been thinking about a mental health center. Ever since we left Texas, I've had a yearnin' to get back into the business of helpin' folks," Mary announced. "Now that Mother has moved in with us and our last child is in college, I need a new challenge," she added softly, her voice cracking, eyes filling with tears.

Silence and a sense of understanding permeated the room as we shut our study books, clasped hands, and bowed our heads for the closing prayer. An invisible cord, an unbreakable bond, encircled our group. Each of us, in our own way, was struggling with personal issues, such as self-esteem, the approaching empty nest, lost dreams, and a sincere desire to make a difference in our world.

"If we're serious about this center, we need a plan. Think about it, and let's talk next week," Mary called over her shoulder as she pushed open the classroom door on that memorable day. She marched to her car, shoulders set with an air of undaunted determination.

And that's how it all began: a small group of midlife women from various backgrounds, with different talents and personalities, following a dream, a vision of a mental health center.

"Okay, ladies, we can sit here forever and discuss the trials and tribulations of our lives and the world. We can have a real pity party. Or we can get excited about having the time and motivation to follow this dream," Mary began the following meeting, lightly pounding on the table to get our attention.

We all quieted as Mary continued. "I called all of the schools in the area regarding a master's program in counseling and asked them to send me a catalog.

Next week, I'll start making personal visits to each college. I may be over fifty, but I'm going back to school!"

Barbara chimed in with statistics regarding our county as being one of the fastest-growing counties in the nation and suggested that she start taking classes in art therapy.

We had the co-captains and cheerleaders for our team. Mary was a woman who made decisions and acted on them, immediately if not sooner. Barbara was a dreamer, an artist, who welcomed new ideas and new challenges. On the other hand, their teammates—Vaneece, Ruth, and I—looked at them with skepticism.

"You're serious about this whole idea?" I asked. "Do you really believe this is possible? Both of you seem to have found your niche. I don't see where the rest of us fit into your dream."

"You gals know my family has to be my top priority right now," Ruth said. "This sounds like a wonderful dream, but with small children at home, I don't know how much time I can to give to this project."

Vaneece sat quietly, lost in her own world of worry about her two teenage sons and their problems. "It does sound like a great project, but I'm just not into sharing your excitement today. Maybe next week."

Suddenly, eight sets of eyes focused on me and I sensed they were waiting for me to get on their bandwagon.

"Where would we get the money?" I asked. The scars from going through a failed family business were fresh in my mind. "My stomach just churns at the thought of going through that experience again." I knew I was throwing a bucket of cold water on their obvious enthusiasm, but at that point in my life, starting a business sounded more like a nightmare than pursuing a dream.

"Oh, come on, Betty," Mary said. "You're the one with the bookkeeping experience. We're going to need a lot of help in that area."

"All right," I hedged, "I'll think about it."

Maybe I do need to do less talkin' and more doin', I thought. *If I start helping others, I'll spend less time feeling sorry for myself and our personal financial problems.*

Out came the flip charts! With each brainstorming session, the enthusiasm grew. With our co-captains leading us, we began speaking to key members of the community, other counseling centers, doctors, pastors, teachers, and business leaders.

"Well, we've been at this for a month now, and I think we're making real progress," Mary commented at one meeting. "I guess the time has come to discuss money, and I have good news. Mother has offered us a loan. What do you think about that?"

Stunned silence filled the room.

I think it's getting too late for me to get out of this, I panicked. "Maybe it's time we get some legal advice," I suggested.

"I've got an appointment with an insurance agent," Mary responded. "I have a feeling that could be a major issue," she said as she rolled her eyes upward and sighed.

During the next few months, the meetings with the insurance representatives and lawyers opened our eyes to the real world and to the potential dangers involved in going forward with our center. We were strongly encouraged to shelve the whole idea, and the discussions with the lawyers resulted in the most difficult decisions we had to make: Should we incorporate as a nonprofit or a for-profit organization? And, last but not least, who was going to run the business?

"Over these last few months, I've spent hours praying about this project," Ruth said.

"First of all, why did we get ourselves into this time-consuming state of confusion in the first place?" Mary asked. "Isn't it because many of the people moving into our community are hurting due to broken relationships, financial setbacks, and substance abuse problems and need somewhere to go for help?

"Mental health centers bring healing and whole-ness to broken lives. If we really want to help folks, profit won't be the main issue," Mary concluded.

"It sounds to me like we agree. We will incor-porate as a nonprofit corporation and proceed accordingly," Barbara said. "Now, what kind of an organizational structure should we have?"

"The consensus seems to be that we need a law-yer, an accountant, a doctor, a minister, an educator, a fundraiser, and an advertising specialist," I offered. "Basically, we're a group of women who specialize in parenting, homemaking, and volunteering."

"Come on, Betty. Where's your confidence?" Mary asked. "We may not have the proper credentials to do every task involved with the center, but I believe we are the women who have been given this mission. So we should be the ones to run the business. Let's find peo-ple who meet those other requirements and form an advisory council, and we'll be the board of directors."

The team agreed. Having those difficult deci-sions made, even I began pursuing the dream with new vigor and determination. The next major hurdle was a location for our center.

One day, as I was visiting with an acquaintance, she asked, "Do you know anyone who's looking for a small house in our little downtown area? I have a rental house that will be vacant next spring."

"I know someone who might be interested," I answered.

As we toured the little house, Barbara suggested the living room as a perfect reception area, the two bedrooms for therapy rooms, and the family room for group meetings.

"Let's sit on the floor and think about this for a minute," I urged, feeling like I was on a runaway train. "You gals do realize that if we sign a lease on this house, we are committed? Up until now, this whole project has been a group of women following a dream. Are we honestly ready to turn this vision into something concrete?" I asked.

Once again, Mary jumped into the conversation. "I'll be ready to see clients after I graduate in the spring, and I've already talked to several therapists who are interested in working here. The money is ready, and I believe our hearts are ready, so what are we waiting for?" she said, giving us her obvious vote.

"The little house with a big heart," Ruth spoke up. "This will be known as the House with a Heart." Another obvious "yes" vote.

"Wow, I can't believe I'm really a part of this project. What a mission!" Vaneece added her vote of approval.

"Sounds to me like you're all ready to go ahead, with or without me. So . . . it's going to be with me," I chuckled, already certain I wanted to vote "yes."

We opened the doors to our "House with a Heart" the following spring, with one licensed therapist and four dedicated volunteers.

Several years later, as we gathered for our weekly meeting in a larger facility, Mary asked, "Do you gals realize that we have served several thousand individuals and families since we opened our doors?"

"We've had some tough decisions to make," Ruth offered.

"It's a good thing we decided to be a nonprofit organization, because we're still barely breaking even," I said as I handed out the latest financial reports.

After thinking for a moment, I added, "No, that's not right. We're more than even, because our bottom line has always been measured in terms of helping others and making dreams come true. Just the other day, one of our steady volunteers became our volunteer coordinator. Now, she's joined that small group of women who had a vision, felt called to action, and 'quit talkin' and started doin'.'"

I smiled at Mary, gave her a hug, and whispered, "Thanks, dear friend."

—*Betty Johnson Dalrymple*

The Coat off Her Back

One cold winter evening, my mom and I were standing just inside the main doors of the Mt. Baker Theatre. We had attended a great concert and were waiting for my husband, Bill, to bring the car around. Usually, I would walk with him, but tonight, since Mom was with us, I waited with her.

The crowds were milling around, as they often do after an event in that theatre. It's a magnificent aged place that has been perfectly restored, and people seem to enjoy socializing there. After a while I noticed a young woman with short, multicolored hair and a stud in the side of her nose watching us. I guessed she was looking at my mom; most people did. Mom was beautiful, even in her seventies, and had a rare sense of style. She preferred to dress up when she went out, no matter what others did. In Bellingham, Washington, where we live, the dress is usually "Northwest casual"—jeans, T-shirt, a down vest, and sandals with socks. That was not for my mom. She wouldn't be caught in sandals and socks if you paid her your year's wages. That night she fit in with the ambiance of the elegant building, wearing a very put-together vintage outfit. As we stood there chatting, I could see the young woman's eyes coming back to Mom again and again. She slowly approached us.

"Excuse me," she said shyly to my mother, "I just want to tell you how great you look in that wonderful coat."

Mom turned toward this unexpected encounter, her deep brown eyes sparkling with interest. The sophisticated coat she was wearing was ankle-length and made from a warm, soft fabric. There was a big jeweled pin on the wide collar. Her gloves and boots were matching leather. Mom looked the girl up and down, appraising her in return.

Smiling approvingly, Mom said, "Thank you. You look pretty great yourself."

Seeing the way the younger woman was dressed, I could tell she appreciated vintage as much as my mother did. They conversed for a few minutes about where they liked to shop and what styles they preferred. Mom introduced herself as Betty Lu and me as her daughter. The girl introduced herself and her boyfriend.

"Do you ever go to Labels?" Mom asked.

"Oh, yes, that is my favorite consignment shop! I love the sale room!"

The boyfriend asked, "Did you get your coat there?"

"No, I brought it with me from Seattle when I moved up here." Then Mom put her hand on her new friend's arm and said, "I'd like you to have this coat."

The other woman's eyes widened. "Oh, no," she said. "I wasn't asking."

"I know you weren't, but I'd really like you to have it. I've had my fun with it. Now it's your turn."

The girl shook her head, although I could see in her eyes she'd rather say yes. "No. I couldn't take the coat right off your back. It wouldn't be right." She laughed, "Besides, it's freezing."

Mom smiled again and made a dismissive gesture with her gloved hand, "Oh, we don't have to do it right now. You give me your phone number. I'll call you and we'll make arrangements."

The younger woman looked at her boyfriend.

He smiled and nodded encouragingly. "Go for it."

The young woman looked at me as if she thought I could talk some sense into my mom. I knew I couldn't. To Mom, this made perfect sense. She had already told the girl her philosophy: once she'd had her fun, she was willing to share.

"She doesn't change her mind once it's made up," I advised. "So you may as well take her up on it."

The younger woman turned slowly back toward my mom. "Really?" she asked. "You would really give me that gorgeous coat?"

Mom nodded and smiled warmly. "Yes, I would."

Just then my husband drove up with the car. He stepped out to help us and right into the middle of the confusion of phone numbers being exchanged and plans being made. He looked at me with raised eyebrows. I smiled and nodded.

A week later, the girl and her boyfriend met my mom at her apartment building and walked away with the coat.

That wasn't the first or the last time I saw my mother literally give the coat off her back to strangers. Or jewelry or handbags or even toys she had bought for her grandchildren. If she saw a child who looked like she could use a toy, Mom would give it away and go back for another one. She wasn't rich, just very kind.

After her grandsons grew up and moved out on their own, she liked to "adopt" other grandsons. This is how it worked: Mom would be downtown in a coffee shop or café. There would be a young man of college age in front of her in line. She would step forward when he was getting ready to pay his bill and say something like, "You remind me so much of my grandson. He lives far away. Can I be your grandma for the day?"

The boy would grin and call her "grandma." Of course, being his grandma meant that she would pay the bill. I've never seen one of them turn her down. Maybe she would run into them again, maybe not. Either way was alright with her—and them. She did this "grandma" game especially with young men she thought might be homeless. What did it mean to them to be noticed and treated that way? I can only speculate.

When Mom gave something away, it wasn't something she didn't want anymore, like many of us might do. It was something she was right in the middle of using—like her clothes or jewelry or money she had set aside for a cup of hot chocolate. I think one of the things she learned from growing up during the Great Depression was that we all need to help one another. No matter what circumstances we find ourselves in, we can cheer each other up and share what we have. That was my mom's most enduring legacy—her ability to light up someone else's day, even a stranger's. And isn't that a wonderful way to make the world a little brighter?

—*Deborah Royal*

An Oasis of Hope
in a Harrowing World

The children massed around us like a swarm of irritating gnats. It took every ounce of self-control not to swat them away. Obnoxious, loud, and boisterous, they shoved tasteless gum and stale candy into our faces—the "goods" they needed to sell in order to survive. They are the children of the streets in the Kurdish stronghold of Diyarbakir, Turkey, and we had come to bring to them sports, food, and fun—a camp where, for once in their lives, they would be allowed to just be kids.

The adventure had begun the day before, a day the rest of the world remembers quite differently, for it was September 11, 2001. On that day, our ragamuffin group rumbled through the parched landscape of Eastern Turkey in a rented van. The entourage included Marc and Jayme, Americans living in Europe; Gretchen, a German who spoke Turkish; my husband Russell, a major in the U.S. Army stationed in the Turkish capitol of Ankara; and myself, along with our three-month-old daughter, Andi. Our plan was to travel to Diyarbikar and work in conjunction with a local social service center there.

As the desert dust settled like a mist around a sagging sun, the frivolity of the fifteen-hour road trip came to an abrupt halt with one phone call.

"It was my office," my husband announced. "Something has happened. They said we need to turn on the radio."

Gretchen quickly succeeded in finding a news station. Her face grew tense as she translated about the airplanes, the World Trade Center, the death and terror we all now remember as "September 11."

The van fell into a morbid silence. I gazed at my baby girl, thinking there must be some mistake. After all, Gretchen was translating from her third language into her second. Surely, she misunderstood. Yes, something bad had happened, but not like she described it. It just couldn't be that bad. Things like that don't happen in America; they happen in other countries. They might happen here in Turkey, but not in the States.

We pulled into a combination gas station and diner to eat and try to get a handle on this world turned upside down. There, CNN Turk blared through the heavy cigarette smoke and the aroma of garlic that dominated the air. Although the Turkish words fell incoherently on our ears, the footage that flashed from the TV screen proved undeniable. Half a world away, we, like all other TV viewers, became eyewitnesses to the horrors of that day.

Marc's and Jayme's backs were up. Their eyes flashed the way an adolescent boy's does when a bully has pushed him one step too far. They spewed forth the kind of rhetoric one would expect from any patriotic, red-blooded American. But then suddenly, my husband Russell quickly silenced them.

"We can't think about this right now," he said, almost grimacing under his own anger. "If I think about it, I will turn this van around and go right back to Ankara. I am an Army guy and I want to fight." His lips were tense as he shook his head in determination. "We can't let even this sideline us. We have to think about the kids."

The kids—yes, that's why we had come. We wanted to give hope to the children of the streets. Travel books on Turkey warn of them when they write of Diyarbiker, describing them like a veritable infestation of petty thieves and pickpockets.

The following morning those children, whom we had previously known only through the pages of books, swarmed around us in flesh and blood, their large, exotic eyes sparkling with curiosity as they inspected us strange foreigners. They kept saying the same phrase over and over again.

"What does that mean?" someone asked.

"They are expressing their condolences for what happened yesterday," Gretchen translated.

We all glanced at each other, taken aback that these poverty-stricken children would even know about such world events.

"They say that they understand if you cannot do the camp for them," our German friend continued. "If you need time to mourn what has happened in your country."

Marc picked up one frail, dirty child and spun him around, then leaned toward Gretchen. "Tell them we want to be here. They are important to us."

The children cheered as we made our way into the ugly concrete building that housed the state-run social service center.

We met with the social workers and then stumbled through the city to lunch with various officials, including the head of the secret police. First impressions would be everything on this awkward day. In this foreign world, the secret police had every right to shut us down and send us home. They needed no reason. Christian-Muslim tensions ran high, and the fact remained that we were Christians.

Christ is what motivated us to reach out to these waifs, these discarded, unwanted children of the streets. And so, having forced the harrowing events of September 11 back into the recesses of our minds, we sat below grape arbors around large iron skillets as we ate our lunch. We chose our words carefully. Gretchen translated them all the more meticulously. And, as we consumed flatbread and lamb, something strange and wonderful happened. Suspicion and distrust began to melt into laughter and genuine affection.

After we ate, the police chief came around the table and picked up baby Andi, lifting her high above his head and gently shaking her until she giggled. "She would make beautiful wife for one of my ten sons!" he announced, only half joking.

Everyone chuckled. But the comment bore more than levity. It represented a connection in which this three-month-old infant had unlocked the door to our unhindered ministry to the children of the streets. A tiny baby had sealed a new level of trust between two very different peoples. The love for children established our common ground.

By the time we returned to the social service center, the temperature soared above 100 degrees and the desert sun baked down upon us. Countless prepubescent ruffians crowded around as we worked to break them up into teams and give them colored uniforms. Each foreigner led his own team of ragged rascals, who would follow him anywhere with chests puffed out, chanting their team name—an endearing trait that became less so when Marc began suffering a common stomach ailment we referred to as the "Turkish trots." As he attempted to deal with uncooperative bowels in a primitive environment, his faithful team of about fifteen eight- to ten-year-olds followed him straight to the outhouse, beating on the door and shouting: *"Aslan, Aslan!* (Lions, Lions!)"

The camp attracted more than 100 street children and some major media outlets as well. A stringer for CNN Turk took our head coach, Jayme, aside to interview him at the end of the camp.

"You are doing much more than a camp here," the journalist commented through a heavy accent.

Jayme fidgeted. *What does he mean?* he wondered. *Does this guy know we are Christians? Is he setting me up?* Indeed, it was a question of concern, for although Turkey is technically a secular state, religious tensions, especially in this region, often reach the breaking point. Jayme stood speechless.

"Ask me why I say that," the reporter prodded.

"Uh, okay." Jayme wondered where this was going. "Why?"

"Because these kids are the ones the radical Muslims try to recruit to raise into their suicide bombers," the young Turk explained. "But if anyone ever asked these kids to bomb Americans, they would refuse, because when your nation was suffering this horrible atrocity, you showed kindness to them. Now, they know the kind of people who are hurt by suicide bombings."

The reporter smiled at Jayme, who stood a little dumbfounded, still processing the words.

"You've given these kids much more than a basketball camp this week," the young Turk continued. "You may have changed their destiny."

Time will unveil whether destinies were truly changed that week by simple acts of kindness. But for the forgotten children in this desert land who participated in our camp, September 11, 2001, will always represent more than impersonal terror worlds away. Now, the suffering has a face. And for those of us who took the children into our arms and hearts, this obscure part of the Muslim world cannot be seen as merely the homeland of an enemy. It will always be remembered as an oasis of hope.

—*Trudy Chun*

The Gratitude Effect

More than a decade ago, when I was working as an interpreter in a large California hospital, I was sent to the bedside of an old man with no family. I was told his name was Melquiades and that he didn't speak English and liked to have stories read to him.

"Call him Mel," the director said.

I never learned his last name, but after all these years, it's a rare week when I don't think of Melquiades. He didn't set out to change me or anyone else. He was not a philanthropist or a volunteer. By the time I met Mel, he was incapable of good deeds in the normal sense. A victim of severe complications from diabetes, he was thin and small, no bigger than an average third grader, and never left his bed. Worse, he was gradually losing body parts to lifesaving amputations. The first time I met him, he had lost a foot. After he was stabilized and able to get around, he was returned to the nursing home where he lived. After several weeks, he was back in the hospital. That time, he lost a larger portion of his leg. Later, there was a crisis with his remaining foot.

When I had no translations to do, I would take a book up to the third floor and read to Mel until I was called away. Our acquaintance didn't last more than a few hours altogether. Yet, he changed the way I look at life.

It is said that when a person is happy, those around him become happier and so do the people around those people, and so on. Happiness, the theory holds, is contagious and ripples outward. I could see that effect in the world around Melquiades. His room was near the nurses' station, and there was a palpable cheerfulness among the staff going in and out. And I felt it whenever I walked into Room 306.

"Ah! *La Señora me ha llegado. Ven. Ven, y sientate.*" He gestured to the chair by the window and asked me to pull back the curtain and let in the sunlight.

I had brought a book, but he didn't ask me to read. He smiled, then looked wistfully out the window, and it was obvious his thoughts were far from the tiny hospital room. So I waited.

After a moment, he began to speak softly in Spanish. "Did I ever tell you about my first wife?"

I shook my head, thinking, *No, not your first or your second or any of your wives. I wonder how many there were!* But, to encourage him to speak what was on his mind, I asked, "Was she beautiful?"

He shook his head. "No, not beautiful, although all women are beautiful in some way. She was not unusual. But she was wonderful. Oh, she was a great one. She was a great one to cook!"

Until I was called to the emergency room, I listened to stories of enchiladas, empanadas, flautas, homemade tortillas, and mole. Mel's gratitude and appreciation for his wife were impressive. I glanced at the tray by his bed: simulated beef on powdered mashed potatoes, green beans that had turned grey. He was not complaining. He was lost in memories of mangoes, papayas, pineapples, and flan. His head was full of delicious treasures, and he drifted off to sleep, smiling.

His last words were, "She was a great one to cook!"

The next time I visited Room 306, Mel was obviously uncomfortable. Both legs were elevated, and there were few ways to move. But when he saw me, his smile was the same as before.

"Ah! *La Señora otra vez! Que gusto de verte!*" He gestured me toward the chair and nodded to the book in my hand.

I read to him for a little while, then noticed the dreamy expression on his face, the nostalgic smile as he looked out the window. I knew another story was coming. I put down the book.

"Did I ever tell you," he asked, "about my partner Ramón?"

I shook my head.

"Oh, he was a great one, a great one to play the guitarrón," he began. "We started a mariachi with three other guys, but Ramón was the heart and soul of our band. He loved music, and he loved to play. He was always working up new numbers, encouraging us to practice. We had those fancy outfits with silver down the legs of our pants and enormous sombreros. We looked great, and we sounded great, too."

His head full of the memories and the music he loved, Mel's eyes started to droop and soon he drifted off to sleep, a peaceful smile on his face.

And so it went. With each visit, he would tell me stories of another friend or family member who was a "great one." Each one a particular quality that impressed him, and he loved to think about it, loved to tell about it. At this time of his life, when he was literally losing parts of his body to a ravaging disease, Mel's head was full of gratitude. When so many would have been self-pitying or complaining, his conversation was joyful, and as a result it was a pleasure to be around him. He taught me that you don't have to do something to change the world; you have to be something.

Not long ago, I was ill for several days. I was stationed on the couch, feeling sorry for myself, when my daughter came to see what she could do for me. I was about to start a litany of complaints, but suddenly changed my mind, recognized my opportunity, and said, "Did I ever tell you about a patient named Melquiades?"

She shook her head.

"Let me tell you about him," I said, suddenly feeling a smile coming on. "He was a great one . . ."

—*Sharon Elwell*

A Lift Up—Not a Handout

Four large eggs are all that I have left between me and starvation. I look inside my refrigerator and see them cradled in their cardboard carton, enticing me to delve into their delicate taste and texture. But I can't. I have already eaten my eggs for the day; I must wait until tomorrow to be able to eat two more.

It isn't high cholesterol or heart problems that prevent me from eating the eggs. It's that those four eggs are all I have to eat for the next two days. I know I have a meal of two fried eggs for tomorrow and for the next day. After that . . . well, I can only hope that I will get the job for which I recently interviewed by then.

At least I have a place to live for now. It is a small house for which I have taken over the rent payment from my brother since he moved out and into his girlfriend's home. The rent is due in a week. If I land a job by then, the landlady will wait for the rent until I get paid. If a job doesn't come through soon, I do have someplace else to go—back to my parent's house. But that is not what I want to do. I want to move forward, not backward. I want to be productive and independent. I do not want to be a charity case who depends on others for basic necessities.

Three months ago, I left my job in Cleveland and moved 250 miles south to be with my parents because my dad was terminally ill. Six weeks later, Dad passed away. I stayed on for a while longer, until Mom accepted Dad's death and was able to carry on. Then, we both decided it was time for me to get on with my life, to find a job and my own place. When I left my mother's house, I had enough money to pay for one month's rent and forty dollars for gas money—enough to get to my brother's and enough to get back to Mom's if my mission here fails. I don't want to fail. I want to stay right where I am and resume my life as it was before Dad became seriously ill. But time is running out.

I remind myself that all is not lost yet. I still have four large eggs; twenty dollars worth of gas to get to a job, if I find one, or back to Mom's, if I don't; and a roof over my head for now. The utilities and phone are still connected, though they are in my brother's name. I begged him to keep them on until I could find a job, at which time he could take them out of his name and I would transfer them to mine. That is my hope. At the rate things are going, my hope is starting to seem more like a pipe dream.

So far, the only job I've been able to find that looks the least bit promising is with a CB radio warehouse, called Commtron. Mr. Owens is the man who interviewed me. He seemed encouraging. I told him I had seen his ad in the newspaper and was willing to work for anything, minimum wage, and could start immediately. I've never been good on job interviews, but Mr. Owens seemed interested in hiring me. I hope he does. But it's been three days since the interview and he hasn't called.

My stomach growls again, and I look at the clock. It is noon—time for my daily walk to dig through trashcans for newspapers. Most people give the newspaper a toss after they've read it, and that's what I am counting on. I need to scour the want ads, and I can't even scratch together enough change to buy a newspaper.

I won't wander far in my search; I can only be gone from 12:00 and 1:00 P.M., when I assume Mr. Owens is on his lunch hour. Every morning between 8:00 and noon and every afternoon between 1:00 and 5:00, I stay close to the phone, so I won't miss his call.

I don't know what I am going to do if he doesn't.

So the job hunt must continue. I stroll along the street, lifting the tops off of neighbors' trashcans and peering inside for a newspaper. Maybe today the want ads will have some jobs available for an almost starving woman.

The first can is stuffed with everything but what I want. I walk to the next one, rip off the top of it, and stare down at a neatly folded newspaper. Seeing it is today's date, I remove it and open it up—only to discover that it contains somebody's vomit. "Yuck!" I shout as I throw it back into the trashcan. Continuing on to the next trashcan, I lift the lid and search until, at the very bottom, I find another newspaper that has been pulled apart but seems to be intact. I'm relieved to find the classified section is there and that it's today's paper.

After walking back to the house, I quickly go through the classifieds—"quickly" because there are so few. None of the jobs advertised are suitable for someone with my qualifications.

I sit on my sofa and stare at the telephone that isn't ringing. With each passing moment, the tension builds. The stress level is making me so hungry that I want to rush to the refrigerator and fry me a couple more eggs. I am hungry. For four days I have survived on two eggs per day. By now, you'd think my body would have adjusted to so little food. It hasn't, and I am hungry.

I'm going to sit here until five o'clock, when I know Mr. Owens' work day at Commtron ends. Then I am going to go search those very same trash-cans for a couple morsels of food that look like they are fit to eat without causing me to die from some deadly contagion.

At about two minutes before five, just as I rise from the sofa to go "dumpster diving" for food, the phone rings. *Oh, my God, the phone. Please let it be Mr. Owens*, I silently pray.

I pluck the receiver from its cradle. "Hello?"

"Miss Hudson, this is Tim Owens from Commtron."

"Oh, hi, Mr. Owens."

"I'm calling to see whether you'd like to come to work for us," he says. "It will be minimum wage and part time. We'll see how things work out. If every-thing goes well, we'll change it to full time and give you a little more money."

"That's great, Mr. Owens. When can I start?"

"Can you come in tomorrow?"

"Yes, sir, I can. Thank you! Thank you so much."

The need for food suddenly leaves me. All I can do is smile and say, *Thank you, thank you, God, thank you.*

I am so anxious and excited, it is hard to sleep.

I rise bright and early to get ready to drive to my newfound job, grateful that I have enough gas in my car to get back and forth to work for a week or so.

When I report for work, I learn that I've been hired as a file clerk to straighten out some extremely awful customer files that a person who has never filed before had totally discombobulated.

"Linda, you know how to file, right?" Mr. Owens asks.

"Yes. You asked me that when we first talked."

"Good. That's what you will be doing for a while. I cannot find anything. If a customer has a question or a complaint, it takes me hours, sometimes days, to find the file. Please start with that file cabinet and begin with the letter A. You'll have to check every file and go through every file drawer and every cabinet, from A to Z, fresh and new."

"Yes, sir."

I work, the lunch hour arrives, and I don't leave.

"Aren't you going to lunch, Linda?" he asks.

"Um, I thought I'd just stay here."

"Well, I'm going to go. You want me to bring you something back?"

"No thanks. I, uh, I'm not very hungry."

"Do you like hamburgers? I'll bring you a hamburger."

"Thank you, Mr. Owens."

He leaves for lunch, and I want to cry. He must have guessed that I don't have any money for food. My stomach is making mild, rumbling noises due to hunger the entire time he is gone.

As soon as he arrives, I snatch the bag he hands to me, rip it open, and try to make myself eat slowly to savor every morsel. I have only two eggs left now, and I don't know when I will get to eat again. I don't know when I will get paid. It's only Wednesday. He watches me and he knows I'm hungry. He walks to the soda machine and comes back with a cold drink that he hands to me.

"Haven't had much to eat for a while, have you?" he says kindly.

"No, I haven't. But now that I'm working, I will survive."

The next day, Mr. Owens brings my lunch again, this time without asking. Later that afternoon, he hands me a check for two days work. After I cash my check, I try to pay him back for the two lunches he bought for me, but he won't accept the money.

After working as a "temp" for a month, I am put on the payroll as a full-time, "permanent" employee. My landlady agrees to wait a few weeks until I have enough money to pay the next month's rent, and I switch the utilities from my brother's to mine.

Because these two strangers took a chance on me and gave me a helping hand, I don't have to return to my mother's home with my tail tucked between my legs—penniless, homeless, and hopeless. Instead, I am happy to get out of bed each morning and go to work for a living, just like my dad taught me to do, with my head held high. What's more, my confidence has returned and once again I believe what my dad always told me—that I can do anything I set my mind to. Suddenly my dream of becoming a teacher, of helping kids reach their dreams, seems within reach.

—*Linda Hudson Hoagland*

Forgiving the Unforgivable

Though it has been more than twenty-five years since my brother's death, I still remember that morning as if it were yesterday. I see in slow motion those first moments when we found out my twenty-two-year-old brother, Gary, had been murdered: Answering the phone. Handing it to my mother. Her collapsing. My father's stricken face. The scene is etched in my memory like a permanent scar.

My brother was a musician who made his living as a drummer in a rock band. A true child of the sixties, Gary wore his hair long, lived each day with the belief that all men were his brothers, and preferred to "make love, not war."

The details we received about the night he died were sketchy. He was killed in a small town in West Virginia, by someone he had once called a friend. The young man and my brother, who were housemates, had argued about something. When the discussion got heated, Gary, who never was one for fighting, said he didn't want to argue and went upstairs to bed.

We've never gotten a true picture of what happened after that. What we do know is this: the young man, high on some substance that was a frequent companion of that lifestyle, either fought with Gary and stabbed him in the neck or crept up on him as he slept and cut his throat. In either case, the results were the same.

The call that changed our lives forever came early in the morning on March 7, 1975. It was the state police calling to tell us my brother had died in an ambulance on the way to the hospital.

Over the next few days funeral arrangements were made and relatives arrived. I was fourteen at the time, the youngest in a family of eight, which in one horrific instant was reduced to seven.

What I remember most is watching my mother. After the call came, she walked all over our three-story house wringing her hands and crying, repeating the serenity prayer over and over. She seemed to be searching for something, and many years later when I asked her what it was, she thought for a moment and then said, "I think I was looking for your brother."

I also watched my mother the night of the wake. I followed her everywhere, needing to be near her. Not many words were spoken between us. What possibly could be said?

I was standing in the vestibule of the funeral home when the funeral director told my mother that she had a telephone call in the office. She looked a bit puzzled but followed him to the phone. I followed her.

After listening to her speak for a few minutes, I had a pretty good idea who the person on the other end was. After she hung up, she confirmed my suspicions and relayed the entire conversation. What she told me changed the way I have viewed life ever since.

The woman calling was the mother of the young man who killed my brother. They lived in another state. She didn't know us and had never met anyone in our family. But she found it within her to track down my mother and tell her how sorry she was for what happened. She said her heart went out to my mom and that she would pray for our family.

What my mother said to her amazes me to this day. She didn't curse this woman for bringing someone into the world who had taken the life of her child. She didn't vent all the rage and pain she must have been feeling on the mother of the man who had murdered her son. She did not thank her politely for calling but reject her apology, telling her she would need time before she would be able to even think about forgiveness.

Instead, my mother said, "My heart goes out to you. I now know where my son is every night. I know he is at peace and will come to no more harm. I will never again have to worry whether he's cold or sick or needs me. Your pain with your son is just beginning. I will keep you both in my prayers."

They exchanged a few more words, and then my mother hung up the phone and went back to the foot of the casket to accept condolences from those who had come to pay their respects to her son. As young as I was, I knew I had just witnessed something rare and beautiful.

That woman had the courage to reach out a hand to my mother, and my mother had the graciousness to accept it. These two women, both engulfed in sorrow, showed compassion such as I have rarely seen since. To this day, I am awed by the woman's courage in apologizing to my mother and humbled by my mother's unhesitating mercy in forgiving the unforgivable.

When the young man's trial was taking place and people were encouraging my mother to fly to West Virginia to make sure the killer got what was coming to him, my mother's heart remained the same. She said she would crawl to West Virginia if it would bring Gary back, but since it wouldn't, she saw no reason to spend her energy making sure someone else suffered.

I don't remember my mother ever lecturing me on the need to forgive others, even when we believe that what they've done is unforgivable. Instead, in a way no words could have, she showed me the need for—and the power of—forgiveness by demonstrating this truth.

I am now a grown woman with grown children of my own. With each passing year, I am more aware of the incredible lesson of forgiveness I witnessed that night. Whenever I hear someone recite a tale of why something that someone has done to them is unforgivable, I remember.

My mother is seventy-five years old. She has fourteen grandchildren and eighteen great-grandchildren. I'm sure, if asked, she would say she has never accomplished anything great in her life, never done anything particularly special. But I would disagree. Although my mother received no awards and no newspaper headlines for what she did, she is a hero nonetheless. And I wonder if it is not these extraordinary acts of forgiveness and kindness by ordinary people that change the world for the better for the rest of us. I know it did for me.

—*Mary Long*

A Better World for $50 or Less

It began with an innocuous request from a candidate for a master's degree in English. Her assignment was to interview someone who had undergone a personal trauma. I agreed to be her subject. She asked, and I answered, many questions pertaining to the situation. She concluded with, "What would you most like to do?"

"I want to do something that matters," I answered, tears spilling over.

"Goodness," she said. "Of all we've talked about today, that was not the question I thought would upset you."

Later that day, I "supposed" a scenario to my husband, John. "Suppose I had tons of money, I didn't have to work, and I had the personality to organize a grand effort of some kind. What would I do?" I said. Then, before he could answer and we could talk it over, I dismissed the idea. "But there's no point in dreaming about it. I can't do it."

John finished pouring fuel into the tractor he was about to take out to cut brush. The large field used to be a cow pasture, when the previous owner of the land was a farmer, which we were not. Still, my husband refused to allow the acres to grow to weed and scrub, and he spent many hours mowing and trimming after his full-time job.

"See that field," he pointed. "If I looked at the whole job at once, I might say it was too much to even try. But a quarter of an acre at a time? That I can do."

Soon after, we launched the "$50 or less plan." Thus began years of putting aside a grand philanthropic plan and thinking of little acts of kindness that were doable.

Neither of us put much stock in gifts to each other. We were adults, after all, and really had what we needed. We preferred to acknowledge a birthday or anniversary with dinner at a favorite restaurant, a visit to an ice cream shop, or simply time. The money we might have spent on gifts went to the new plan, and we took turns coming up with something helpful to do for others. It was much more fun than shopping for a present we didn't really need.

There were three rules to the plan: (1) Most of what we chose to do had to cost $50 or less. (2) Whenever possible, we were to be anonymous. (3) Rather than merely writing checks to national charities, we would concentrate on the local community.

The opportunities were endless. John bought a gift certificate to a local grocery store and mailed it—anonymously, of course—to a family that had suffered a house fire. That was the first of many such certificates that went to local families who were trying their best and needed a little lift to keep their heads above water.

I left a box of craft supplies and coloring books at a preschool known to take children from needy families at much reduced rates. John went out in his truck late on winter nights to plow and clean out the heavy piles of snow that blocked driveways after the town plows had passed. I've pulled weeds around the memorial at the fire hall; though not quite anonymous, few people noticed what I was doing.

Once, we heard a neighbor's chain saw as he labored to cut up a tree that had fallen on his lawn during a storm. By the time my husband and I had serviced our own saws and driven the half mile to the house, the neighbor family had taken a break and gone out, we presumed, for supper. Working as feverishly as the shoemaker's elves, we cut and stacked, and then disappeared before the homeowners came back. That was a tiring hour, but such fun! They eventually figured out who had done the chore, but it took a while and we tried to put on innocent faces when we were confronted.

There were things to do that cost nothing. In summer, a home on a country road had a large colorful flower garden that increased in size and diversity each year. Sometimes I'd see someone pulling weeds, watering the plot, or planting a new lily. At a different home that I passed daily, the owner made a cute Halloween display of eight little, white-cloth ghosts holding hands in a circle around a tree. They made me smile. In each case, an anonymous note taped to the door let the homeowner know that they had contributed to someone's pleasure that day.

Extra produce from our garden and grape vines disappeared when piled at the end of our driveway with a "Free" sign on the box—except for the year when everyone had so many zucchini and pumpkins that I could have sworn there were more of the gourds when we got home at night than we had left there in the morning!

We bought T-shirts and socks for the residents of a veterans' home, leaving the packages at the post office that served as a collection point. When I copied a holiday newspaper article about the year-round needs of the elderly veterans at the facility and posted it in the window of our business, it paid the most amazing dividends. A customer saw the wish list and decided to crochet some lap robes, as requested by the veterans' home and the VA hospital. When we put up another poster requesting yarn scraps, it resulted in a deluge of material. I sorted yarns by thickness and color, and Rita crocheted more than twenty lap robes and neck pillows for local military veterans that year.

It has been many years since the day I lamented about not being able to do "something that mattered." I can't build a college on a reservation in Montana, but I can give a modest scholarship to a student brave enough to take out a loan for his education. When the news of hardships on the other side the country or the state tug at my conscience and I feel inadequate for not being Bill Gates or for not having the resources of a great foundation at my disposal, I go back to the day when my husband said, "Take it a quarter of an acre at a time." Then, it's easy to find something doable to do that matters— especially when that quarter acre is within my view.

—*Ann Vitale*

In Lila's Shoes

For the better part of a day, I am walking in Lila's shoes. Literally.

Her shoes are knee-high black rubber boots, and I wear them as I walk through a valley in the Magdelena region of Colombia to investigate a murder. Christian Peacemaker Teams, the organization I volunteer for, has been asked to provide an international presence while government officials gather evidence.

For over fifty years Colombia has been wrenched by civil war. The ensuing violence is not simple to understand, because multiple armed actors, as they are called in Colombia, have fought over land, oil, drugs, and power. The fighting has been divided between three groups—the Colombian National Army, guerrilla forces, and paramilitary organizations—but factions exist within them. The FARC and the ELN, the two largest guerrilla forces, have fought each other to control territory. In addition, there is collusion between groups. Currently, allegations of connections between government leaders and paramilitaries are under investigation.

Trapped in this net of violence, the people of Colombia struggle to live out their daily lives. Christian Peacemaker Teams (CPT), which seeks to transform lethal conflicts through bringing a nonviolent presence to volatile areas, has been working in Colombia since 2001. A full-time team of six to eight people, supplemented by a much larger group of part-timers like myself, support threatened communities in the Magdelena Medio region.

In the case of this murder, a *campesino* (small farmer) organization has asked CPT to provide international accompaniment. Trust between the government and its citizens, particularly poor, rural Colombians, is already low, and there is suspicion that the government investigation will favor the army. Such requests are typical CPT work: having an outside witness in a conflict is one strategy to encourage fairness in honoring the law and to defuse the potential for additional violence.

It is challenging to decide which requests to take on. There is always more work to do than resources allow. When this particular request arrived, two full-time team members were on vacation and two others were off working with another community. Those remaining were relatively recent arrivals with less CPT–Colombia experience. I volunteered to go with other teammates, but knew I would probably quickly be in over my head; my Spanish was rusty and I was still adjusting to the heat.

We had been told we would travel by truck and motorized canoe, so when we get to the small village of Puerto Matilde and learn we will be walking on a muddy path through the jungle for an hour after crossing the river, I know we're in trouble. Although it is not the rainy season, we had a torrential rain the day before, and when Colombians say mud, they mean serious mud, thick and swampy.

As I stand under the small awning at the dock, I look around me: everyone but my teammates and I have on the standard campo rubber boots. The *campesinos*, of course, know how to dress for this weather, but the human rights workers from the city are wearing boots, too.

A woman notices my gym shoes and says in Spanish, "Don't you like boots?"

"*No lo tengo*," I say hesitantly, unsure if I've used the object pronoun well enough so she will get the point: I don't have any.

"What size do you wear?" she responds in Spanish.

"*Ocho.*" Eight.

"*Ocho?*" She stares at my foot.

I'm not sure how to respond. Doesn't my foot look like a size eight? "*Y usted?*" I fumble, asking for her shoe size, trying to figure out where I've gotten off track.

"*Treinta y tres.*"

I peer at her boot . . . thirty-three? Clearly, we're not using the same system.

While we guess at my shoe size, a slender woman in a red blouse approaches. She points to the boots on her feet and gestures toward me. At first I'm hesitant. Won't she need the boots herself? But after a few exchanges, I understand: the woman, Lila, is staying in Puerto Matilde and offering me her boots for the expedition.

I pull off my gym shoe and, feeling a bit like Cinderella, slip my foot into her boot. "*Perfecto!*" I exclaim, and they truly are, sturdy, hitting me just above mid-calf, and snug enough so they won't easily slip off when the muck slurps at my feet. "Are you sure it's okay?" I ask in my halting Spanish.

Smiling, Lila nods and tugs off the other boot.

I bend down and slip her coffee-colored foot into my gym shoe. It seems to fit.

Lila puts on the other shoe, stands up, walks across the cement slab. I notice the shoes aren't tied.

It crosses my mind that Lila may never have owned shoes with laces, so I kneel down and tie these North American shoes on her South American feet. Lila pats my head.

Someone shouts that the canoe is boarding. I hop down to the riverbank. A man from the *campesino* group we are accompanying offers his hand to steady me as I step over the gunnel, and then we're off, zooming down the river. A second canoe carries the soldiers and the government officials who will investigate the murder.

Starting out, we walk together in a line. We are an odd mix: government officials in black uniforms; Colombian soldiers in camouflage, automatic weapons slung across their backs; several female lawyers representing different sides of the investigation; local and regional men and women from *campesino* organizations; a young boy in a peach-colored shirt; CPTers with our blue vests and red hats.

Although it is hot and humid, as it nearly always is in this part of the world, I am grateful for the overcast sky as we trudge through the muck. Without the blaring sun, the temperature has been turned down a notch. The walk has enough challenges from the terrain alone. The recent rains have turned the caramel-colored soil into a soupy mush. Sometimes the muck is over a foot deep, viscous enough to suck boots off your feet. Fortunately, Lila's boots fit snugly. Still, even with boots, this unstable landscape can be treacherous, the mud slippery, the depth of standing water unknown. Barbed wire fences line the path, waiting to snag us.

Our earlier line disintegrates into small groups of three or four as we make our way through this swamp. Finally, we reach a small river. The current is strong, but just across lies our destination, the small house where Aicardo Antonio Ortiz once lived. A few take off their boots and wade across. I take my chances. The water comes within an inch of my boot rim but does not spill over.

The officials divide us into two groups—soldiers near the house and civilians within the corral—and the murder investigation begins. One of the officials sets up her note-taking station on the civilian side to get the testimony of neighbors who heard the shots, while the other officials gather around the house. I stay with the civilians, still keeping an eye on the government workers with their yellow tape measure moving around the house. It is not a story easily measured out. Only the most basic facts are unequivocal: on July 8 soldiers from the Colombian National Army killed Aicardo Antonio Ortiz, a rural man in his fifties.

Other pieces of the story contradict each other; the army tells one version, the civilians another. The army contends that Aicardo was part of the guerrilla forces; the community believes otherwise: how could he be a guerrilla with a son in the Colombian military? The Army reports three *guerrilleros* were with him who escaped; the villagers say he was alone. According to the soldiers, the shots were part of a spray of fire coming from the hillside; according to the family who lives across the corral, no other shots were fired. The army claims Aicardo came out of his house shooting; neighbors insist he was unarmed. In the army version, Aicardo died outside the house; community witnesses say he died in the house. The army says the body had a radio and a grenade near it; the community says the body had been tampered with by the time the authorities arrived.

But my teammates and I are not there to assess the truth of any version. Rather, we have been asked to accompany the local *campesino* association to make sure their perspectives are heard.

Across the fence, the ballistics expert continues to take measurements from different angles. A group of soldiers stick together by the creek. The rest of us crowd under the shade of the single tree in the yard, our bodies limp from the heat. A neighbor brings us a jug of *limonada*, a small sip for everyone.

At last, when the official investigation around the house finishes, the civilians are invited to view the site. The house is raised on stilts, the ladder a halved tree trunk. I climb the rungs slowly and cross the rough planks that serve as a porch. How does one enter a space marked by murder?

As I step into the meager, one-room house, my first instinct is to look for signs of life: what does this space tell me about the man who lived here? From the doorway I look across the room and see the simple plank bed, the dishes hung from the wall, the small television set on a shelf, the light blue shirt on the hook beside me: a whole life in this one room. But I can't avoid looking down, where the signs of death are splattered. The entire floor is stained with a long splotch of red, a kind of nebula splattered from the door to the bed. In the center of the dark wood, there's a jagged hole where a bullet ripped through the floor. I walk carefully, trying to keep Lila's boots from getting bloody, but it is impossible to be in this house and not walk on blood.

The sun fades. It has been a long day. We walk back through the muck, re-cross the river, and get out at the port, where Lila is waiting for me. Her boots are crusted with mud, and I attempt, in my fumbling Spanish, to apologize for not cleaning them. She squeezes my hand.

I think about the life Lila walks in: the armed soldiers she passes daily in her town, the potential for blood spilled. As a civilian in a war zone, simply walking down the street carries risk. The dirt streets and small, unpainted houses suggest additional risks that come with poor rural life in Colombia: lack of clean water, limited access to health care and education, few employment options.

As a woman from the United States, I know I cannot fully understand what it means to walk in Lila's shoes, but I am grateful for the gift of a day in her boots. A local human-rights advocate tells us that today's investigation was more thorough than usual. While I would like to think this is due to my team's presence, there are no certainties in Colombia's complex conflicts. Yet, with the help of locals like Lila, I believe we can bend the arc of the universe towards justice. As I slip back into my shoes, I can feel the heat from Lila's feet, a heat that accompanies me all the way home.

—Carol Tyx

Some names in the story have been changed to protect the privacy of those individuals and their families.

Touching Souls

Last October while vacationing in Hungary I visited the Jewish Museum in Budapest. As my tour group approached the museum, we came upon a cluster of high school students waiting on the sidewalk. Conversing in a mixture of English and German, they wore sweatshirts emblazoned with "Heilige Nacht" in Gothic print.

Their leader, a middle-aged nun, called them together as our guide led us into a garden. The students, restless and energetic, were laughing and joking. Our groups merged, and I found myself standing next to the nun, whose wavy blond hair peeked out from beneath her white-bordered veil.

When we stopped in front of the memorials to the Righteous Christians, a girl turned to her. "Sister Catherine," she exclaimed in English, "there's a memorial to the Swedish diplomat, Raoul Wallenberg, whom we've read about."

"Yes, but look at the list on this wall," the boy behind her added. "Many others tried to save Jews."

I must have looked reflective, even sad, because Sister Catherine turned to me.

"Did you lose family or friends during the war?" she asked.

"No, I didn't," I replied. "I was just thinking that it must be very difficult to bring German students to this museum."

"Our headmaster insists that our students understand history beyond what their textbooks teach them," she told me, her blue eyes turning somber. "Yes, it is difficult, but it is necessary. They must realize that all people are capable of evil. But the dreadful evil of our own country's past must never happen again," she said. Then, she sighed before adding, "At least in this Jewish Museum, the Christians who tried to save Jews are recognized and honored."

We turned as our guide pointed to a large metallic sculpture of a tree. "The American actor, Tony Curtis, donated this sculpture of a willow tree to our museum in memory of his father," she told us.

Several students blinked as they recognized the name. Although they belonged to a younger generation, many had seen reruns or DVDs of Tony Curtis' films.

"*Some Like It Hot*," a boy said with a grin.

"Have you seen *The Vikings?*" another asked.

"No, but I saw *The Chastity Belt*," a girl replied. Her comment created a flurry of girlish giggles.

"I saw Tony Curtis once in a film, maybe twenty years ago," Sister Catherine told them. "It was called *Welcome to Germany.*"

Just then the guide added, "Tony Curtis is Jewish. His real name is Bernard Schwartz."

The students looked confused.

"Does that surprise you?" the guide asked them.

"Yes," a tall young man admitted. "I thought of him as being . . . just American."

She smiled. "*Just* American? America is a country of immigrants from many countries."

The young man shifted his weight. "Still, I wouldn't have thought—"

His hesitation was followed by laughter.

"Tony Curtis' parents emigrated from Hungary in the 1920s, yet Tony memorialized the thousands of Hungarian Jews who remained in Hungary," the guide explained. "Each silver leaf you see was engraved with the name of a person who was murdered during the Nazi period."

When she paused, several students stepped forward to read a name or to photograph a leaf. Stepping back, they wore solemn expressions.

"Huge numbers of people killed are only statistics to them," Sister Catherine said softly as she turned to me. "But see their reaction to a single name on a leaf? It touches their souls."

I knew that in addition to his acting career Tony Curtis is also a recognized artist. As I looked at his representation of a weeping willow, I saw that the three closely aligned trunks represent an inverted menorah. Two curved branches on both sides of the central trunk stretch outward; silver leaves cascade from slender boughs. A gentle breeze caused the leaves to sway; to shimmer in the sunlight. In motion, the leaves transformed the weeping willow into a tree of life.

"Why are there stones at the base of the tree?" a girl asked.

"The stones symbolize continuing prayers," the guide replied.

The students' mood was thoughtful as our guide took them into the magnificent Dohany Synagogue. Leaving, they were silent as she led them past the section of ghetto wall topped by "razor" barbed wire that is adjacent to the museum. Somberly, they continued on until they stood in front of the tombstones that mark the mass graves in the Martyrs' Cemetery.

Entering the Jewish Museum, the students observed rooms filled with exhibits of Passover and ritual objects. Once we were inside the room commemorating World

War II, I realized that some of the students were well aware of that period and much of what it meant. I overheard their comments: several still had grandparents and older relatives who had attended classes with Jewish teachers or had friends and neighbors who had left the country or "disappeared."

Tony Curtis' name came up again. They were struck that this Hollywood actor, who seemed more current to them than their grandparents, had also been affected by the Holocaust. They looked perplexed, and I sensed that connecting that sad period in Germany to a larger-than-life person whose film adventures they had followed was disconcerting.

When I returned to my home in Massachusetts, I contacted Tony Curtis, asking if he had designed the Memorial Tree himself and if he wished to comment on his endeavor.

He replied with a handwritten note: "My father, Manuel Schwartz, used to go to the Dohany as a young man, and I wanted his name to be remembered. I chose the Dohany Garden and designed the Memorial Tree to be remembered, always, as my father's soul."

In further correspondence, Mr. Curtis made a distinction between who the tree memorialized and to whom it was dedicated. "The tree is dedicated," he wrote, "for all people to come and see."

All people.

I remembered Sister Catherine's words: *Huge numbers of people killed are only statistics to them, but names on the leaves of the Memorial Tree touch their souls.* I realized that, in connecting human names to that horrifying past, those young people had gained insight and empathy that they would carry with them out into the world, like seeds on the wind. And that is how good will toward others, toward all people, takes root and grows—with understanding and compassion.

—*Eleanor Roth*

Guardian Angels

"Star light. Star bright. First star I see tonight."
That was how I began my nightly prayer ritual when I was a young child. While kneeling beside my bed, I would choose the brightest star I could see and make my wish. Then I would pray for God to bless and care for my loved ones.

The Christmas Eve I was five years old our house was full of company, and at bedtime I had to surrender the bottom of the bunk bed to sleep on a cot upstairs all alone. My mother knew I was both nervous and excited, so she came up to get me settled in. She got down on her knees with me, and when I began my usual ritual she listened closely to hear my wish, which was to be safe and unafraid in the dark all alone. Mom interrupted before I started my prayers.

She told me to look again at the star I had just wished on. I had already been told about heaven and angels and where my Grandma, Grandpa, and Baba went when they died, but that night Mom told me about a very special angel. She told me that, from then on when I looked to the stars, I should direct my wishes to Robert.

Robert? I had a guardian angel named Robert?

My mother explained that before she married my dad she had been married to a wonderful man named Mike McKenzie. With him, she had a baby boy they named Robert. He was born in December, but tragically, he had died that Christmas Eve. The very next Christmas Eve, my mother's husband was killed instantly in a horrific head-on train crash. She told me that sadness revisited her each Christmas Eve, but the love and joy that we kids and Dad brought to her life eased her pain. It made me feel better knowing we gave my mother some comfort. We cried, grieved, and prayed together. I fell sound asleep, feeling safe and comforted that night and for many other nights, knowing about my guardian angel.

Then, the year I turned seven, another Robert came into my life. About eleven years old, he had Down's syndrome and was placed in our second-grade classroom experimentally. We bonded instantly. Robert sat in the seat in front of me so I could help him with his work. He became very reliant on me and would make a fuss if he couldn't stand next to me in line or keep me in sight at recess.

One day I fell in the schoolyard before the morning bell rang. My knees were skinned and bleeding badly, and I was weeping. Out of nowhere, Robert scooped me up into his arms and carried me off. The teachers were slightly alarmed and yelled at him to put me down, but I couldn't see what they were concerned about. I felt quite safe. Robert was much bigger than the other kids and able to push past everyone to march me into the building, directly to the school office. Robert walked right up to the startled principal and laid me down on the desk.

"Fix her!" he demanded loudly. "She's my friend!"

That Christmas, our school put on a pageant and invited the parents to come on the afternoon of Christmas Eve to watch it. Our class performed the nativity scene, with Mary, Joseph, shepherds, the three wise men, and an angel who stood out front to narrate the story. Miss Stone chose me to play the angel. I figured it was because I was a good reader and had long curly hair and cherub cheeks. I was ecstatic!

My mother made me a beautiful costume with delicate wings and a golden halo. While she fitted and sewed the costume, we talked more about my guardian angel. I told her a theory I had, that perhaps her baby Robert had not died. I felt sure there had to have been a mistake at the hospital and that the Robert in my classroom was really her child all grown up. I tried to reassure her; although he was different and lived in a special place, Robert was still being my guardian angel and I loved him.

She reminded me that we had often visited her baby's grave and told me I should be very thankful to have two Roberts watching out for me.

Every day before the pageant, my class rehearsed our nativity scene. I loved every minute of it—except for one thing: Robert wasn't able to have a speaking part. He would play a shepherd seated on the floor with a scratchy, gray, woolen blanket pulled over his head and body with only his face revealed. That made me sad, but Robert didn't seem to mind at all. In fact, he took his role very seriously. When he was supposed to stand up, he stood up; when he was supposed to sit down, he sat down. The only problem was that he desperately wanted to be closer to me.

During the course of every rehearsal, Robert would creep over to wherever I stood and play his part seated on the floor near me. Miss Stone explained over and over to him how important his part was but that it must be played from the proper position. He said he understood and continued to be a wonderful shepherd, but only when he scooted forward on his blanketed behind and stayed front and center with me.

I would take him back to his spot and sit with him a while, but to no avail. He was just too nervous on the crowded stage without me in his sight.

Two days before Christmas Eve, Miss Stone paid a visit to our house after school. *What on Earth had I done wrong?* I worried. I'd never heard of a teacher coming to someone's house before.

Mom and Miss Stone called me into the room. They wanted to know what I thought we should do about Robert. With serious faces, they told me I had a big decision to make. They said that, whatever I decided, they would understand and stand by me. I could be the Christmas angel and stand out front of the nativity to narrate the play, in which case Robert would have to be kept out of the production completely because he refused to stay in his shepherd's position. Or I could give up my role and the costume of the angel to someone else and sit in the back under one of those heavy blankets playing the part of a shepherd with Robert so he could still participate. What a weight to place on the shoulders of a seven-year-old.

Many years have passed since then. I still have a fascination with the stars. I still gaze at the brightest ones and think of my guardian angels, which now include all my loved ones who've left this world, among them my dear mother, who died suddenly at Christmastime, too, when I was only seventeen. My wish every Christmas Eve is that they all know how grateful I am for their presence in my life and for their outstanding guidance. I also pray that Robert knew how thankful I was for his unequivocal friendship when we held hands under our scratchy, gray, woolen blankets all those Christmas Eves ago.

—*Lea Ellen Yarmill Reburn*

A Little Can Be a Lot

I grew up thinking my mother was a sucker. She answered every request, whether it was from one of my whiney sisters or brothers, our next-door neighbor, or the endless number of charities who routinely mailed donation requests to her. Then there was the time my mother cut our lunch plans short to buy a couple of hamburgers for a homeless guy in the middle of downtown San Francisco.

We were on vacation, just the two of us, staying with my older sister who lived in the city. To be traveling with my mom was a rare treat for me. Not only because I was eighteen and just starting college, but also because she didn't take my father or any of my other six sisters and brothers, who all stayed at home in Iowa. She took only me.

My mom and I were standing at a "don't cross" traffic signal. A crowd of stalled pedestrians stood around us, and a disheveled man sat at the corner begging for money. He slurred his words, and at his side was a paper bag crumpled around the shape of a bottle with only the rim exposed. His filthy clothes hung limply over his lean figure, and the smell of urine made me hold my breath, repulsed. We all pretended to ignore him—that is, everyone but my mother.

Looking him straight in the eye, Mom asked him matter-of-factly, "If I give you money, then are you going to go and buy alcohol?" Right in front of all those people, she asked this.

The man couldn't quite meet my mother's eyes when he answered, "No, ma'am. I don't drink." He turned his head from side to side as if the emphasis would convince her that the thought had never entered his mind. Then he added more quietly, as if explaining himself, "Just need a li'l food, that's all."

Mom looked around and noticed a McDonald's sign above us. "You want a burger?" she asked.

I wanted to drag my mother away, peel her from the curious eyes of all those onlookers. The man would undoubtedly refuse my mother's offer. He wanted money, after all, not cheap burgers. He stalled, looked uncomfortable—maybe because he was surprised she hadn't ignored him or just tossed him a coin like most people, all the tourists like us, people in business attire, and locals who passed him by, most barely noticing his existence. Instead, my mother had spoken to him, asked him a question, and was waiting for his answer.

"Okay. Sure. I wouldn't mind a burger," he replied sheepishly.

So my mother marched inside to order the food, with me following along behind. Another mother might well have done the same: Set a good example for her daughter. Shown her that giving to those less fortunate was the compassionate thing to do. Taught that it is unfair to judge—that people have flaws and make mistakes, that bad things happen to good people, that some people are merely making do. But, honestly, what difference would my mother possibly make in this man's life? I knew any kind of answer from my mother would be complicated. To a man who probably received more disdain than charity, my mother giving food amounted to a small act of kindness. Her insinuating he'd rather drink than eat, though, meant she recognized his weakness, that he was a human being who made mistakes, just like everyone else. Only, my mother wasn't about to feed an addiction, to further a wrong—not if she could help it, not if she could help right a wrong.

For as long as I can remember, my mother has tried to help others. She answered all of the mail from charities. She sent five- and ten-dollar checks to UNICEF, to the local women's shelter, to organizations that sponsored a child in one African country or another. I swear, someone must have put her on a central mailing list, because a new donation plea seemed to show up in my parents' mailbox every month, always asking for money. The checks she wrote were small, because she didn't really have any money to spare, not with eight children to feed, clothe, and care for with only my father's paycheck, and not a big paycheck at that. But she couldn't say no, not to anyone in need.

Following my mother into the McDonald's restaurant that day in San Francisco, I told her the man probably wasn't hungry, that whatever she was going to buy him would hardly make a dent in his day.

"It's good to help," she had said simply.

It was the same answer she'd given me before, each time I'd told her that ten bucks would hardly make a difference to that charity or the other, so why keep writing check after check?

"It's good to help."

She didn't say anything about her past, when she had lived in need herself, during all those years of hunger and fear during World War II that she never forgot. My mother had been eight years old when she crawled past a barbed wire in the dark, hardly daring to breathe. Her family was trying to cross the border, to escape the soldiers who'd come in and taken over her house and her town in Eastern Europe. My grandmother put their lives on the line because she was determined to lead her six children from certain hell toward a chance at a better future. Only, for six years after that night, they found themselves in another kind of misery.

They lived side-by-side in a single building with other families, all refugees. Living quarters were separated by blankets they hung like walls, offering no privacy, not enough space, and little comfort. Four of them crowded into a single bed to sleep. My mother lay at the foot of the bed, poked, prodded, and smelling her siblings' feet all night long. The food was bad, when they got it, and paltry, barely enough for all of them. So they searched for mushrooms or berries in the nearby forest. In the winter, they scrounged for food in the dump outside of town, searching for half-eaten morsels of other people's thrown-away scraps.

Their living conditions brought other suffering, too. One year my mother and her brother Alex came down with typhus. Alex nearly died. They were quarantined in the hospital, and my mother slept alone for a whole month. No visitors were allowed, which was worse than smelly feet for a shy young girl who didn't speak German.

During those years, an American lady used to send her money and boxes of clothing. She never met the woman, but my mother would reply with letters of thanks, telling the lady about her life in the camp. Then my mother's family received word that they would get visas to leave the camp and go to the United States. My mother never heard from the lady again. But my mother never forgot her or her kindness.

As I watched my mother hand the man at the corner a bag of cheeseburgers, I realized she saw herself in him, in each person she gave to. Her past motivated her to do what she did day to day, giving what she could to charities, to loved ones, and to strangers like the hungry homeless man on the streets of San Francisco. Her motto—"It's good to help"—reflected how she saw the world: Some have less; some have more. And, sometimes, the merest stroke of luck separates the haves from the have-nots. It's up to those who have to help those who have not. And even a little bit can help.

"Be thankful, Elizabeth," she could have told me that day. But she didn't. My mother was a woman of action, not of admonition. In fact, I didn't recognize until much later that what she did that day in San Francisco made a difference. It made a difference in me.

—*Elizabeth Sharpe*

One Less to Count Up

A guard buzzed us through the front gate. We swiped our identity badges, signed for our personal protection (panic) alarms, or "PPAs," and stepped into "holding." After placing our bags on the conveyor of the X-ray machine, we emptied our pockets into the personals trays and walked through the metal detector to collect them at the other end. I punched my code into the pad on cabinet B, removed my keys, and joined Sue, who was waiting for me at the door leading to the yard. Although I had traveled this route many times, I still flinched at the electric buzz of the security doors unlocking and the clunk of the automatic locks setting behind us. The yard gate slid open, and Sue and I hurried along the snowy path, shoulders hunched against the January cold, making our way across the open courtyard to "J block"—a.k.a. "the school"—at the Willow Creek Correctional Institution.

"The Creek" is a medium-security penal facility for adult offenders. Operated by the Canadian government, it houses offenders designated as "less dangerous" who have been transferred in from maximum-security prisons. The inmate population is all male and representative of virtually every cultural group in Canada's very multicultural society. Inuits from the high Arctic and First Nations' people from northern reserves do time with urban blacks and Latinos from the Caribbean and South America. The Asian countries and eastern and central Europe are equally well represented, along with both English- and French-speaking Canadians. Their offenses range from fraud to murder, and their release dates vary from months to decades. White-collar professionals mix with assembly line and construction workers, bike gang members, and those who have never held a job. Young, middle-aged, elderly—all had two things in common: they were in prison and they were our students.

We card-swiped ourselves into J block and the teachers' office. The first order of business was to test our PPAs. No guards are stationed in our halls or classrooms; they are on the "ranges" supervising the nonattending prisoners. If one of us instructors felt threatened or if a problem arose among the inmates, we would push the red call button on our PPAs and the guards would come running, literally. I called the central station, pushed my panic button, and the guard confirmed that my alarm was active.

It was the start of another teaching day at "prison school." I was in today as a substitute teacher. Sue was a regular. She was on contract to service students with special needs. Her primary job was to provide programming for inmates in "seg"—system speak for "segregation," solitary confinement, or in prisoner parlance, "the hole."

Sue and I had worked together years ago as colleagues in a large, rural public school. I left that school to assume a principalship elsewhere. Sue went on to devote the last decade of her teaching career to working with children who had special needs. We had stayed in touch, sharing our trials and triumphs over the years, and we retired from the public school system within months of each other. I graduated to the golf course, but Sue wanted to keep her toe in the educational pool, so when Willow Creek needed staff, she accepted the challenge of working with adult offenders who had special learning needs. A valuable addition to their staff, she was soon asked to take on the daunting task of teaching in the hole.

The routine in seg is very strict. Sue's students are escorted from their cells by guards to meet with her at a small table in the glassed-in exercise room.

There, between the stationary bike and the weight bench, while an observing guard stands by on the outside looking in, Sue instructs her pupils. During a typical visit she picks up completed assignments, teaches new concepts, and hands out fresh materials. Depending on time and circumstance, she sees two or three seg students a visit, before returning to teach classes in J block. If there is a lock-down, she is denied entry; if a lock-down occurs while she is in seg, Sue, too, is locked down for the duration.

The school runs year round. Summer vacation is meaningless to students who can't go anywhere. Nobody really graduates, but many earn their high school equivalency diplomas on the "inside."

When Sue first called me to fill in for her, I was a little hesitant. Oh, I had joked with her about the perks of prison teaching: no interfering parents, classroom discipline backed up by armed guards, and really long after-school detentions. But actually going inside to do it was intimidating. After some jitters during my initial visits, I became comfortable with my work and agreed to join the very short list of replacement teachers willing to work inside.

Today I would be teaching an English as a second language class. I turned to prompt Sue to test her PPA and found her studying an inter-facility courier envelope. It was addressed to her and marked personal.

This was unusual. The transfer of records was a controlled process within the prison and personal mail was an exception. Sue pressed her panic button, and she, too, was activated. She began opening her mail, and I sat at the desk beside her to review notes left by the teacher I was replacing.

The two-tone signal of the public address system sounded and a disembodied voice commanded, "Count up! Count up!" That was the cue for prisoners to be mustered on the ranges. If the count was correct, our inmate/students would be released to come to class. I made a crack about bad counts being our school's equivalent of a snow day, but Sue didn't laugh. She was focused on the papers she had removed from the envelope. Her face was flushed, and she seemed on the verge of tears.

"Sue, what is it?" I asked.

After a moment she replied, "Do you remember Shawn Reynolds? You taught him in seg when you filled in for me, when I had my surgery last year. You know, the good-looking young kid who spoke English well enough, except for his habit of using profanity as an adjective."

I smiled. I did remember him. I had spent a week helping him learn "f---ing" fractions.

Sue began by telling me Shawn's story, how he had been transferred to the Creek from Kingston, but had lasted only two days on his range. On the outside, he had some big-time drug connections, and his reputation followed him here. When he refused to cooperate with his "brothers" on the inside, he was beaten, twice. The warden ordered Shawn to be relocated to seg for his own protection.

"A lot of my students in seg want to work with me just to fight the boredom. I'm human contact, a chance for conversation and news from the outside. Others really want to learn. I wasn't sure into which category Shawn would fall," Sue said.

Like most of our guys, Shawn had been unsuccessful in the public school system and had a very low opinion of school, teachers, and his own ability to learn. His behavior and his extracurricular activities with a youth gang had gotten him expelled from high school, eight credits short of graduation.

"At our first meeting, he told me that what had happened since his arrival had convinced him to try and turn his life around. He wanted to get his high school diploma to help him succeed when he got out," continued Sue. That was a tall order for someone in seg. "But Shawn seemed genuine, so I did some testing, developed a plan to suit his goals, and we got started."

Math was Shawn's biggest problem, as I knew from my stint with him. He had missed many of the basics and started out working on seventh- and eighth-grade material.

"Adult learners with fragile egos don't like doing 'kiddie' math, but we got over that hump and he began to roll. Every time I visited, he handed in completed units for marking and requested more," said Sue.

The guards reported that he would work well into the night and sometimes all night. He wore down pencils and used up calculator batteries. He completed his assignments, made his corrections, and did well on his term tests.

As per regulations, Susan had stood outside watching through the window of the exercise room when Shawn completed, and passed, his first final exam! One credit down. Only seven "f---ing" credits to go. That was two years ago.

Susan and Shawn kept at it, and although there were some bumps in the road and frustrating delays and restrictions, by last March Shawn had finished five more credits. He had just two more to go to achieve his high school equivalency and get his diploma. At that pace, he just might be finished for fall convocation.

"On the Thursday before Easter break, there was a lock-down and I couldn't get in to see him. But I arranged for the guards to deliver the outlines and texts for the new courses to his cell, so he could look them over while I was on holiday," Sue said. "When I arrived in seg on Tuesday, Shawn was gone. The only thing the guards could tell me was that he had been removed by executive order and returned to solitary in maximum at Kingston. I was devastated. He—we—were so close to reaching his goal. I never heard from him again. It was like he never existed."

Sue paused.

"And? . . ." I prompted.

She handed me the contents of the envelope. It was a photocopy of an official province of Ontario high school diploma. Printed boldly in calligraphic script on the title line was the name "Shawn Reynolds." Dated October 2002, it was sealed and signed by the Minister of Education for the province. There was a handwritten note clipped to it, which read:

"Sue, Thank you so much for helping me and believing in me. (even when I didn't). You've got the patients of a Saint! (ha, ha!!) You're awesome Sue and I'll never forget you and how you so deeply made an impact on my life. Just knowing you is a privilege I'm very pleased to have. Very warmest regards, Shawn R. Reynolds."

The signal tone of the PA system broke the silence and the voice announced, "Count's good!

Count's good!" Our students were being released to come to class. It was time to go to work.

Flashing Sue a big smile and a thumb's up, I dropped the papers on her desk and headed off to meet my class. She was already on the telephone to seg, checking to see if she could get in to see her regulars and if there were any new arrivals. Who knows how many more Shawns are in there? Would that we had enough Sues.

—John Forrest

The names of the prison facilities and the names of some of the people in the story have been changed to protect the privacy of those individuals and their families.

Stepping Out of My Comfort Zone

It was my lunch hour, and I needed to hurry if I was to return in time for my one o'clock meeting. Nassau Street was crowded with shoppers, all with similar agendas: grab a quick bite to eat while running as many errands as could possibly be jammed into a sixty-minute period. Located in the heart of the Financial District of New York City, Nassau Street is a shoppers' mecca that is blocked off to vehicles during mid-day hours. Monday through Friday, the routine remains unchanged as tens of thousands of pedestrians spill out of towering office buildings onto a vast outdoor mall to eat and shop, and then eat and shop some more. Cliques of people stride two and three abreast, discussing everything from world peace to the lunch selection of the day.

I had several things to accomplish in less than an hour: eat, pick up a few things from the drugstore, and exchange a pair of shoes I had purchased the day before. Easy enough if I just stayed focused. Deciding what to eat was no simple task. Choices along Nassau and the intersecting streets included Japanese sushi, Chinese lo mein, American barbecue, Italian pizza, Spanish empanadas, Greek deli, and of course, every other fast-food place imaginable. It's all within walking distance of Wall Street, for New York is, after all, America's great melting pot. I purchased a slice of pizza to eat on the run.

The cashier's line at the drugstore was long, and I tapped my foot impatiently as I inched toward the register. From there, I trotted one block over and exchanged the shoes for a half-size larger. My errands finally completed, I glanced at my watch. Just in time; my lunch hour was over.

As I hurried through the crowds back to the office, a young woman stepped out from one of the many boutiques lining the cobblestone street. I'm not sure why I noticed her; there was nothing about her that was outstanding. Of average height, she wore a light coat with deep, square patch pockets, and she carried a large shopping bag from the boutique in her hand as well as a handbag slung over her left shoulder. She had almost melted into the crowd in front of me when a man appeared, also directly in front of me. He wouldn't have caught my attention except that he seemed quite focused on the woman. He strode up directly behind her and immediately began to match his steps with hers.

People jostled each other in both directions on the sidewalk, and the crowd threatened to hide the man tailing the woman from my view. I craned my neck to keep the pair in sight. Something was going on here, although I wasn't sure what. He kept his pace and then sped up a bit to shorten the distance between him and the woman. She was apparently oblivious to his presence. They were a strange couple, bound together, yet not together.

My gaze was now riveted on this unlikely duo. I'm usually so engrossed in my own thoughts and schedule that I'm oblivious to my surroundings, but this time my curiosity was piqued. I quickened my pace in response. The meeting would have to wait. Continuing to close the gap between them, he matched her steps—left, right, left, right—falling in line directly behind her. Then, as he eased from behind to beside the woman, he carefully reached out in front of him to slide his right hand into the large right pocket of her coat. When his hand reappeared, he was holding her wallet. It all happened in a New York minute, yet I felt suspended in time, the sole observer of a movie being filmed for my own individual viewing. *This must be what it feels like to be omniscient*, I thought.

I walked faster, pushing past people in front of me. Why was I the only one to notice the unfolding drama? My adrenaline flowed as I shouted, "Hey! You! That's not yours! Give it back!"

Heads turned from all directions to stare at me, but at that moment I didn't care what they thought. I only cared about these two strangers.

They both turned as one to look at me, and I frantically shouted again, "That's not yours! Give it back!"

When the woman glanced at me, her expression reflected a typical New York reaction: *Oh no, here comes another character.* But then, in that same moment, she realized the man beside her was standing unusually close and holding what appeared to be her wallet. Her look instantly changed to one of stark confusion.

Meanwhile, the thief froze in his tracks, a moment of indecision that would cost him his plunder. The icing on the cake, however, was his unmitigated gall. As I stepped forward, he glared at me and exclaimed, "Why don't you mind your own business!" Now that's New York chutzpah! In the next instant, he hastily handed her the wallet, muttering, "You dropped this," before he darted into the crowd and was quickly lost from our view.

The woman looked down at her wallet, puzzled by the turn of events.

I took a step closer to her. "You didn't drop your wallet; he took it out of your pocket. He must have been in the store and saw you place it there."

She nodded, still obviously confused, as she put her wallet where it belonged and then gripped her purse tightly. We parted company, two strangers in the big city, returning to our respective jobs and routines.

Hurrying back to the office, I reflected on the little drama that had just taken place. I had stepped out of my comfort zone into what felt like a Hollywood movie, and the movie had a happy ending. The woman got her wallet back. And I learned something that would stay with me forever: one person *can* make a difference.

—Ava Pennington

Upon a Midnight Clear

I used to be a pessimist. I not only saw the glass as half-empty, I thought there was something floating in it, too. It took a silver Pontiac Trans-Am and a little, old bookstore owner to show me how to find and embrace my inner optimist.

In December 1984, I was falling apart, along with the rest of my young family. America was in the grips of a recession. In the La Mesa neighborhood of San Diego, California, where we lived, the cost of living was high and jobs were hard to find. My husband, Brad, had been out of work for months. His unemployment was running out, and so far he'd been unable to find a new position. We were desperate, not to mention in danger of having the Trans-Am repossessed. I was trained as a teacher, but our two boys were preschoolers and I was pregnant again. Plus, although I didn't know it then, I was having twins and was feeling doubly sick in the mornings and dead-tired each afternoon. Still, when I heard about a temporary clerk position at a nearby bookstore, I applied and was hired by a nice, older lady named Katy Woods. She had never married and wore a shapeless dress and stiff black "grandma" shoes.

"I need extra help for the Christmas rush," Katy said. "But I can only pay you a dollar-fifty per hour."

The next day, I brought a baggie of saltine crackers to nibble in case morning sickness overcame me. I wore comfortable shoes and didn't worry about the boys; their father would take good care of them. The three of them drove me to the bookstore in our last remaining possession—a fancy, late-model, silver Pontiac Trans-Am Firebird. Brad had bought it in better times, but now, with its steep monthly payments, it felt like a half-ton burden. Family members had already chided us for not selling the car, but the nationwide recession made for a soft used car market. Nobody could afford to buy it from us for what we owed on it. Besides, I had to have transportation to get to work; San Diego bus services were patchy at best, and I was too pregnant to pedal a bike up and down the La Mesa hills.

The store bustled with Christmas shoppers, many asking for books I'd never heard of. It had been years since I'd operated a cash register or made change.

Still, I loved being around books all day, even if I had to dust them during slow times.

By the time I received my first paycheck, I'd made several new friends and could at least buy a few groceries. But the car payment loomed, already overdue. Friends and family were unable to help. We had nothing left to sell. The car finance company had issued several warning calls and letters, and we dreaded every knock on the door.

I was pessimistic as usual. "We'll never get the money together in time," I complained, rubbing my swollen feet. "Our goose is burnt to a crisp."

Brad, a hardworking ex-Marine, shook his head. He put a finger to his lips, and glanced at our boys playing on the rug, and whispered, "Something will come up."

"I hope it isn't my lunch," I groaned, laying a hand on my growing belly.

He smiled. "You know what I mean. Don't be such a pessimist."

I blamed my worry on hormones and tried hard to keep the boys from hearing about our woes. Their grandparents would provide them with Christmas presents, of course. The kids knew we were struggling, though, and kept their letters to Santa Claus short. Their sense of sacrifice made me proud but also a little sad.

On Christmas Eve I reported for work, prepared to deal with last-minute crowds of shoppers. In our inland suburb, we rarely felt breezes from the Pacific Ocean, but that day cold marine winds nipped at my cheeks. The forecast was for rain. The gloomy overcast sky matched my mood. I had few gifts for my children, the cupboards were nearly bare, and any day—no, any minute—the car company would arrive to take the Trans-Am. I scolded myself for dwelling on the negative, but it was hard not to brood. Tears stung my eyes.

Brad poked his head out the open car window. "Think positive," he said.

The boys yelled, "Merry Christmas, Mom!"

I couldn't resist smiling. "I love you," I shouted over the rumble of the muscle-car engine. The Firebird emblem reminded me of the mythic Phoenix rising from the ashes. "Might as well say good-bye to you, Pontiac," I muttered, waving as they drove off.

Inside the bookstore, I quickly donned my clerk's smock and hurried behind the counter.

During a brief lull, the owner, Miss Katy Woods, made a rare appearance on the sales floor and asked me to come to her office. My legs shook as I imagined the worst: the "temporary" job was over and I was being let go. Great. A real nice Christmas gift.

Katy, in her frumpy dress and cardigan sweater, sat behind her desk. With her still-black hair secured in a bun and owlish glasses perched on her nose, she reminded me of a typical spinster.

"Sit down," she said.

I thought, *Oh no, here it comes.*

"We wish we could keep everyone we've hired for Christmas," she began. "But I've had to make some difficult decisions."

I swallowed the lump in my throat. "Of course."

She smiled. "I've decided to offer you a full-time position. That is, if you want it."

I couldn't hide my surprise, but I nodded.

She stood and beckoned me to follow her to the children's section of the store. "Pick out some books for your little boys. For Christmas."

I must have gasped. "You're kidding?"

She frowned. "And be sure they're good, hard-bound books, too."

She pulled several children's volumes from the shelves. I juggled the stack of books, barely able to hold back my tears.

"Miss Woods, how can I ever thank you?"

"Call me Katy."

"I mean, Katy. You've been so generous; I don't know where to begin . . . ."

"I nearly forgot." She reached into her sweater pocket, drew out a sealed, legal-sized envelope, and laid it on top of the stack of books in my arms. "Don't open this until you get home."

Her old-maid shoes clunked as she strode back to her office. I stood there, stunned.

I was relieved when Brad picked me up. The Trans Am was still ours—for now. I could hardly wait to tell him of my job offer and the Christmas gifts for the boys. The sealed envelope in my purse almost screamed at me to open it. But I'd promised to wait.

Two hours later, the boys were safely tucked in bed and Brad and I sat at the table.

"You won't believe this," I said, pulling the envelope from my bag.

Before I could explain, a loud knock on the door made me jump.

Brad frowned. "I'll get it."

Two burly men stood outside, demanding we hand over either the payment or our car.

Brad turned around to look at me as I ripped open Katy's envelope. Inside, the exact amount we needed lay in crisp new bills. Even the repo men admitted they'd never seen anything like it. They accepted our money, and by the time we closed the door, both Brad and I were crying. I told him about the job, the books for our kids, and the kindness of one slightly nebbish bookstore owner.

In the morning, we celebrated Christmas. After the boys opened their gifts, Brad and I sat together watching them play. He turned to me.

"Sorry I don't have a gift for you," he said. "I still don't know how I'll find a job."

I grinned at him, certain my trademark pessimism had changed into a sunnier attitude. "Don't worry, honey," I said. "Something will come up."

—*Linda S. Clare*

Frugality: It's Not Just about Penny-Pinching Anymore

That cliché of the mid-twentieth century, "There are children starving in China," originated in the kitchen of my childhood home I'm certain. When my mother attempted to shame us with that information, my daring, smart-mouthed older brother occasionally pointed out that, whether the last bite of peas on his plate went into his stomach or our garbage, it had no chance of benefiting Chinese kids.

"Well, then, why don't we just pack this stuff up and send it over there?" he'd suggest. "I'm sure they'd like my leftover peas."

Feeling safe with my head bowed toward my empty plate, I'd snicker a muffled agreement.

Those gray-green canned peas on his plate mingled with a smudge of orange French dressing and a smear of chicken gravy looked disgusting; nonetheless, he was encouraged to eat them. In my childhood home, waste was a grave offense and an affront to my parents, who lived by lessons learned during the Great Depression. Even though the 1950s were marked by a sense of plenty, they never took a well-stocked cupboard for granted. If even a few tablespoons of some component of a meal remained uneaten, my mom put it into a Pyrex custard bowl and covered it with a saucer. She knew someone would scarf it up later.

After the dishes were done, my brother and I plunked down in the living room to watch TV before returning to the kitchen to do our homework. That was when I'd pull open the heavy door of the seafoam-green Frigidaire and find a tiny Pyrex bowl holding two dozen kernels of canned corn in a puddle of its accompanying sweet-salty liquid. I'd carefully set it over the pilot light of the matching green gas range, which coaxed the chill from it while I scratched out my arithmetic assignment at the kitchen table. Sometimes, a plate with two tomato slices left from dinner sat on the beige linoleum kitchen counter. One was always an outside slice, rounded on the bottom and held intact by its skin. This slice I found irresistible. It was perfectly neat for picking up without making a mess, and because it was the smallest slice it could be angled into my mouth in one bite.

When I wasn't in my school uniform, my outfits were usually second-hand. My mother bought much of our clothing at the Next-to-New shop in downtown St. Paul. She and her sister Emma nicknamed it "The Shoppe" and compared their bargains with pride and delight.

"Whadja pay for that?" one of them would taunt.

The other would brag, "*Piten da stinto*"—or something like that, speaking in Slovenian, their secret language. My cousin Kathy, Emma's other niece, eventually figured out that this meant a quarter.

The Goodwill and Salvation Army stores were Mom's and Aunt Emma's next favorite clothing destinations. Emma could tailor nearly anything into a good fit, and she taught me to shorten pant, skirt, and sleeve hems while I was still in grade school. Hardly a compliant pupil, I grumbled with every pull of the needle and thread.

When I was fifteen, my mother and I took the red and yellow city bus downtown to The Shoppe one Saturday morning to buy my first prom dress. Reluctantly, I accompanied her over the creaky wood floor to the back of the dingy establishment. A well-heeled, stylishly coiffed Junior League volunteer clerk directed us to a rack crammed with formal gowns of every length and pastel color. My cranky sulk dissipated as I examined the grand array of dresses; I chose a flouncy formal of starchy white organza trimmed in pale pink satin to try on. Behind the crimson and aqua floral curtain of the tiny dressing room, I rejoiced at its perfect fit.

Because I was not eager to disclose to my friends that I dressed in the used clothing of strangers, I always mumbled complaints to my girlfriends that I wore my cousin's hand-me-downs. This white lie served me well, so they assumed my prom dress was one Kathy had worn a few years back. In truth, most of Kathy's clothes were too challenging to tailor to my size, even for Emma, since Kathy was five inches taller and a couple pounds thinner than I. Emma soon taught me to use a sewing machine, and I fashioned my own prom dresses for the remainder of my high school years.

In general, everything in our home that could be reused was reused. This included tiny brown glass bottles from prescription medications, cardboard cereal boxes and their waxed paper inserts, plastic bread bags and their twisty ties. My mother saved the envelopes from our bills, using the backs for writing telephone messages or grocery lists. Cardboard boxes full of empty cans from vegetables, tomato juice, and coffee were stacked downstairs in the furnace room and later used in painting or varnishing projects or to hold worms dug up for fishing bait.

Countless bundles of brown paper grocery bags from Red Owl were tied with twine and stored out in the garage next to bins of empty glass jars. Department store gift boxes were treasures that filled a basement closet.

Most of these parsimonious measures made at least some sense to me, but there was one practice that I judged to be beyond reason. Every time my mother unloaded a package of paper napkins after grocery shopping, my job was to get the heavy steel scissors from our kitchen drawer and cut along the main fold of each, making two napkins from one. Aggravated, I would cut a half dozen napkins at a time with that dull scissor, ensuring that each thinner napkin would be a trapezoid with one chewed up edge rather than the tidy, single-folded square my mother intended. This chore repulsed me; I thought it was boring, stupid, and embarrassingly penny-pinching. Further, I loathed using the flimsy, jagged-edged, two-ply napkins that resulted. I was mortified when a friend eating at our home reached for a napkin.

When I matured and established my own household, I shook off that Depression-era mentality faster than the crash of the stock market that precipitated it. I reveled in the eschewing of those childhood rules. As a young adult, I adopted a standard of living that

was comfortably situated between frugal and luxurious. It was sensible; it felt just right.

Now middle-aged and long past that miserly
childhood, I sometimes reminisce with my husband about my youth and marvel at how effectively
I've broken free of the penny-pinching ways of my
parents.

"Hmmm . . . I'm not so sure about that," Mike
said the last time we had this conversation. Smiling,
he continued, "I don't think I know anyone who
does as careful a job as you do at straightening out
grocery store twisties."

I cringed as I pictured the glass votive holder in
my kitchen cupboard, neatly packed with straight,
flat, green twisty ties that are perfectly good for
another twist or two. Of course, I reuse office paper
printed on one side either by running it through
my printer on the other side or as scratch paper on
our kitchen desk. And it's not like I hoard Classico
spaghetti sauce jars; I just like to keep two or three
dozen of them down in the furnace room to store
extra paint. They're also great for storing leftover
soup in the fridge or uncooked rice in the cupboard.
Furthermore, my two cardboard boxes of Planters
peanut cans and Kemps cottage cheese cartons . . .
well, everyone knows how useful those can be. And
those capacious cardboard boxes fit nicely under the

basement shelves, where I store gift and shoe boxes, too.

"Okay," I replied sheepishly. "I am pretty thrifty, but I'm not miserly."

As the twenty-first century unfolds, it appears that my thrift may be an adaptive trait. The sagging economy and concerns about the environment have made frugality both fashionable and beneficial. In this new, more "conscious" way of living, the lessons I learned from my mother have taken on new meaning. Being thrifty, consuming less, recycling, and reusing stuff not only benefits individual households, these actions also benefit people around the globe and the planet itself.

My friend Carol and I walk to a nearby coffee shop every Monday morning. This week, while hiking to our destination, we discussed our efforts to stay healthy, spend modestly, and live "green."

"Conserving is actually pretty painless," she commented.

"Yeah. For me, it's like coming full circle. There's a different goal today from what it was in my childhood, but what we do to get there is really much the same."

Both Carol and I are steering away from storing our food in plastic, not only because we fear the presence of carcinogens but also because of the energy spent producing them and the sometimes nondegradable and environmentally harmful waste those containers add to the landfills. Carol's gone back to using Pyrex; I'm reusing jars from spaghetti sauce and peanut butter as often as I can.

As we waited for coffee, we chuckled about the great quality of the bargain clothing we now have time to ferret out at second-hand stores since we've both retired.

"Who knew we could be such fashionistas in recycled duds?" Carol asked, reminding me of our recent trip to the Salvation Army store.

It was my turn to buy our drinks at the Java Train, so I stood at the counter waiting to place my order. Carol strolled over to a cart across the cafe to get water and napkins and to claim our usual spot. I arrived at the table with our coffees just as she placed a glass of water at each end of the tiny table that wobbled slightly when she set them down. As I lowered myself into a chair, I saw her unfold a huge paper napkin. She tore it in half and laid one jagged-edged piece beside each coffee mug.

—Beverly Golberg

No Prescription Needed

Sometimes the medicine you need doesn't fit in a pill bottle.

It had been a month of loss and tears for me. My husband's Alzheimer's had progressed to the point that I had to place him in a nursing home. But even as the sympathy flowers began to wilt on my dining room table, I had begun to see that, compared to the struggles of other people, I had it pretty good. I was healthy, I had devoted friends, and as I set off to run errands and do a little shopping, I had some extra cash in my pocket.

People seemed to be having trouble everywhere I went that day. The postal clerk was alone and over-worked. She apologized for taking so long. "That's okay," I said.

The checker at the department store could not get the computer to print the correct sale price for my new jacket. As people lined up behind me, she called over the loudspeaker for another checker. No one came. Then, when the computer complied, it charged me twice for the jacket, so she had to call a manager to straighten things out. When no one responded to her first call, she called again.

"I hope that sounded irritated enough but not too much," she said with a wicked grin.

"Just right," I replied, smiling back.

She thanked me for my patience.

"That's okay," I said.

When I left the store with my bag of treasures, all on sale, all purchased with birthday gift money, the sun was finally out after days of rain, hail, thunder, and even some snow. As I walked across the parking lot, I noticed a car of the variety I'm plotting to buy. With no salesman to bother me, I walked around it, studying the seats, the upholstery, the storage areas. Just the thought of driving a brand new vehicle made me smile.

Then, after dumping my bags in the trunk of my old car, I walked across the street toward the pharmacy behind a couple of giggling teenagers running to Taco Bell. They were out-of-towners who came to the coast for spring break. When the stoplight button spoke in a male voice that said, "Wait," they burst out laughing. "It talks!" said the one with the orange T-shirt.

The pharmacy is not such a happy place. Too few workers, too many customers. At least half the time, people coming to pick up pills are told they will have to wait another hour or another day. I have seen senior citizens give back the medication they need when the clerk tells them the price, and no, their insurance does not cover it, or that the co-pay is more than they can afford to pay. I have sat and waited, feeling sick and miserable, watching the minutes tick away. But I was reasonably confident that my thyroid pills would be there. I had learned the secret: call the pharmacy and tell them you want the pills that day, then show up two or three days later. Of course, that doesn't work if you've just come from the doctor with a new prescription.

An angular octogenarian from my church sat frowning on a bench to my left. A young woman in a green army jacket stood at the counter gesturing wildly as she discussed her missing prescription with the pony-tailed clerk. Off to the right, where three chairs sit around a TV screen that runs perpetual pharmacy ads, a white-haired man with swollen ankles groused about how he spent all his time waiting these days. An hour in one doctor's office, another hour in the other doctor's office, and now an hour here at the pharmacy. He was sick of it. The woman next to him, pressing her hand against her belly as if it hurt badly, nodded, trying to be polite. She was waiting for medicine so that her doctor could give her an injection, she said.

The old man noticed me listening and addressed his comments my way. I nodded sympathetically, hoping a stranger would do the same for my father back in California; he spent plenty of time waiting for doctors and prescriptions, too.

The stylishly dressed woman in front of me, whose white hair showed a few last remnants of blonde, turned to comment on the wait. I was surprised to see an oxygen tube stuck in her nose. Yes, it was going to be a while, I agreed. No, it shouldn't be that way. Oh, I was lucky to be feeling better, even if this stupid long wait had taken the bounce out of my getaway day.

Suddenly, the store manager came up to the woman holding her stomach and whispered something in her ear. She covered her eyes and burst into tears. First, I thought they couldn't provide her medicine. But then, when she exclaimed, "God bless him! He was such a nice man," I was certain someone had died.

Aware that everyone was watching, she explained. A stranger, whom she had been telling how much she would love to have a massage chair like the one she was sitting in, had bought one for her. "I don't even know his name. I can't believe it," she kept saying, gazing in wonder at the big box the store manager had set beside her.

The gloom of the pharmacy lifted. The old man smiled. Even the lady from church looked almost happy.

I thought about the many things people had done for me lately, including home repairs for which they refused payment, gifts of daffodils and rosemary, and calls from women I barely knew, asking how I was.

The woman with the oxygen tank made it to the counter. She had ordered three prescriptions for "Harry." They had only one ready.

"That's okay. I'll come back in a couple of days," she said.

My thyroid pills were there. Did I need to talk to the pharmacist about my medication? No, I'd been taking them forever. I smiled. The clerk smiled back.

I wished the old man and the young woman good luck and walked out into the sun, swinging my little white pharmacy bag, marveling at the blessings of good health, good friends, and the generosity of strangers.

—*Sue Fagalde Lick*

The Real Santa Claus

My mom has always been an ardent believer in the importance of generosity, and her secret passion is anonymous giving. From the time I was little, Mom invited me into her world.

For many years we baked cupcakes together each Christmastime to give to local firefighters who had to work the holiday. We'd drive to the firehouse, and when I was old enough, Mom would have me go to the door alone while she watched from the family Volvo. As I presented a surprised firefighter with a tray of sugary goodness, I'd say my carefully rehearsed line, "These are for you because you have to work on Christmas day." I would scurry back to the car quickly, because we weren't supposed to reveal our identities. I remember one year a firefighter turned away, cupcake plate in hand, and called out to his crew, "It's that lady with the cupcakes again!" Of course, people these days usually don't eat unidentified baked goods, but back in the 1970s, people weren't as concerned. They accepted her cupcakes gladly, and we got to experience the rush of making people happy.

After my mother married my stepdad, Barney, she taught him the joy of anonymous giving. He became an eager adherent to her guiding force. Together, they give throughout the year, whether they're driving donated furniture to disaster victims or buying food gift certificates to give to homeless people. Best of all is their special tradition, their annual Giving Day. Each December 22nd, the two of them take the day off work to give gifts to people in need. Although the date is my stepdad's birthday, the focus is not on him but on bringing joy to others. It doesn't matter to them that the day's expenses put a crimp in their already small budget. My mother firmly believes that's what money is for—to help people less blessed than she is—and that one needn't be wealthy to find the resources to give.

The ritual begins the same every year. After my stepdad opens his birthday presents, he and my mom head off to a diner for breakfast. While enjoying their meal, they scan the other tables until they spot someone who is eating alone and looking sad or lonely. Then, with the help of their server, they secretly pay for the person's meal. After they've gone and their server is clearing the table, he or she finds a $50 restaurant gift card with a note that says, "Now you can have somebody wait on you."

From there they go to an outdoor-supply store to buy as many sturdy, cold-weather sleeping bags as they can afford. While checking out, they give the clerk one of the $5 McDonald's gift certificates they carry throughout the day to hand out to anyone playing even the smallest part in their day of giving. After a mountain of snuggly sleeping bags is tossed into Barney's pickup truck, they drive to a shelter dedicated to serving homeless teens. There, they donate the sleeping bags along with other supplies, like thick, warm socks or toiletries stored in festive drawstring bags handmade by my mother.

Next, it's time to go to the abused women's shelter and the shelter for homeless families, where they deliver big, fluffy stuffed animals for the children and supplies for the adults. Their hearts guide them in what to provide, be it canned hams and fruit or soap and paper towels. After these quick, anonymous visits that leave startled social workers awash in a wake of gifts, it's time for the big event. Every year it's something different. Mom and Barney design their annual project ahead of time, brainstorming ideas, settling on one, and preparing.

Recently, I asked my mom which of her past projects stood out as a favorite.

"It was the time we were able to anonymously give a bicycle to someone who really needed it," she said. "We knew it was meant to give away because we'd won it. The universe helps us know what to do."

My mom and stepdad's adventure began when my stepdad saw the cheerful, bright-yellow bike with pink striping one November day. He was in a shop that was sponsoring a prize drawing for the bike, and he knew he had to enter. After all, his and Mom's policy is to enter contests often, because if they win, the prize becomes a gift to give away. Barney's good intentions must have nudged karma, because he won the drawing. It was perfect for Giving Day.

Mom and he were trying to decide who should get the bike when Mom's friend, Lisa, told her about Emily. Lisa had just become a "big sister" to Emily through a mentoring program. Emily was an under-privileged sixteen-year-old who lived with her single mother and little brother in a bad area of town. After school, Emily went to her job at a Burger King, and sometimes she was assigned the closing shift. Because her mother worked nights as a bartender, Emily had to walk home alone after 11:00 P.M. The nearly three-mile trip took her through dark, dangerous streets. Hearing this, my mom realized her special Giving Day project for that year had presented itself perfectly: Emily needed that bike.

Mom bought reflectors, a horn, a basket, and a strong lock for the bike. She thought of Emily's little brother, about ten years old, and decided he'd need something too, so she bought an electronic handheld game. Into the bike's new basket went the boy's gift with his name on it as well as a typed card for Emily: "This is for you because you are loved. I want you to be safe when you come home from your job, and this will help you get home quicker. Someday, you may want to do something nice for someone else, and you can call yourself Santa.— Santa Claus." A big red bow on the basket finished off the surprise.

On the big day, Barney called Emily to make sure she would be home to get the bike. "Hello," he said. "This is the North Pole Delivery Service. Will someone be home at one o'clock to accept a delivery?"

Emily answered with a mistrustful, tentative yes.

Just before the appointed hour, my parents drove to Emily's neighborhood and parked around the corner, out of sight. Barney wheeled the bicycle toward a dilapidated house with peeling green paint and carried it up the stairs to the porch. Emily answered the door.

"I'm from the North Pole Delivery Service," Barney said authoritatively. "Are you Emily?"

Emily said yes.

"This is for you," he said, pushing the bike into the house.

Emily's little brother ran in and saw the gift in the bike's basket. As Barney handed him the gift, his eyes lit up.

"Oh, wow! This is for *me!*" the boy exclaimed.

Before Emily could ask questions, Barney hurried out the door and down the block, leaving behind a stunned teenage girl and her thrilled little brother.

Days later, my mom asked her friend Lisa how Emily was doing. Emily had told Lisa about the bicycle and how her mom was showing the gift card to everyone at the bar, trying to figure out the giver's identity. "She's just sure it's from one of her regular customers," Emily had said, "but nobody will fess up."

Mom was happy that her secret was secure but even happier to hear that Emily was now enjoying safer trips home from work in less than half the time it had taken before. It was hard to tell who was more delighted by the experience, Emily and her family or my parents.

It's fitting that over years of being married to my mother, my ruddy-cheeked stepdad has cultivated the look of Santa Claus, growing an authentic white beard, allowing himself a few extra pounds, and even tagging his red pickup truck with license plates that say, "Sleigh." In fact, he's stopped year round by children eager to talk to Santa. When they approach them, he gives a "ho, ho, ho" laugh and hands them one of the candy canes he always carries in his pockets, be it December or June. My mother stands quietly to the side, smiling and watching. She has no wish to call herself Mrs. Claus; she prefers her quiet anonymity.

Still, as I watch her watch "Santa" and the children, I know a secret those children don't: my mother is the original Santa, the source of the goodness that comes from my stepfather and from me. Mom has always been a force of generosity, teaching me charity and kindness since even before that very first batch of firefighters' cupcakes. When she married my stepfather, she nurtured those values in him too. I know that long after she's gone, her generous spirit will survive in me, in Barney, and in the many others she has touched with her kindness.

—*Alaina Smith*

Some names in the story have been changed to protect the privacy of those individuals and their families.

Bangles, Bubbles, and Blue-Collar Kindness

The summer before I started college, in the early 1960s, I went to work in a glass plant that manufactured bottles and jars in all shapes and sizes for various products, such as catsup, bleach, soft drinks, etc. It was a huge place that was very hot in the summer, and the dress code was cool and casual. Women wore shorts, loose blouses, and sandals, and the men, especially those who worked up where the glass was liquefied at high temperatures, were allowed to dress as comfortably as they wished, short of nudity.

My job consisted of standing at a conveyor belt inspecting the bottoms of Clorox bottles, looking for a certain number. If the number did not appear, the bottle was tossed into a huge bin to my right. If the number was on the bottle bottom, it continued down the belt and was placed into a cardboard container and taken elsewhere. I never found out where the bottles went from there. The job wasn't very stimulating. Conversation with the person at the next conveyor was impossible because of the high noise level, so one had to amuse oneself by occasionally glancing up at the half-dressed men with their bare muscular chests or letting one's mind wander to other things.

The woman who worked on the other side of the conveyor belt from me apparently let her mind wander a bit farther than the rest of us. Her name was Charlene, but she said her friends called her "Charlie." She was a delightfully sweet person who called everyone "dearie" or "kid" in a high, screechy voice that took some getting used to. She constantly chewed on a massive wad of pink bubble gum, and she was always willing to help newcomers learn the ropes.

We worked the swing shift—3:00 to 11:00 P.M.— and the first time I saw Charlene I thought she was going to a party after work. She had on an off-the-shoulder peasant blouse, which she wore way off the shoulder; a very tight red linen skirt, which I was sure prevented her from sitting down; very high-heeled, white, sparkly sandals; and jewelry that looked like she had made a killing at a giant claw machine. Her bangle bracelets, which adorned both arms almost to her elbows, were always clanging metallically against each other whenever she moved, which was all the time at the conveyor belt. Her earrings would have been a huge hit at a gypsy convention. Each day she would appear dressed to the nines, often in a semi-formal or cocktail dress, sometimes topped off with a boa, no less. I don't think I ever saw her in the same outfit twice, and each seemed more elegant than the last.

I came to suspect that the lovely Charlene wasn't playing with a full deck. She was in her mid-forties, had frizzy, long, blond hair of questionable origin, a very nice figure, and had worked at the plant for twenty-five years. With my vast seventeen-year-old wisdom, I wondered how anyone with an I.Q. of even room temperature could look at bleach bottle bottoms for twenty-five years. I mused that only someone who was essentially brain dead could spend eight hours a day, five days a week, for a quarter of a century (and counting) at such a mundane, dead-end, unrewarding job.

One evening during our lunch break, I asked Charlie why she dressed so nicely just to come to work. She giggled and explained that the job was so boring that while she worked she fantasized about the outfit she would wear the next day and pretended she wasn't going to work at all but to a party.

At home, she spent several hours a day planning her ensemble—color coordinating her bag, shoes, and accessories, depending on what type of imaginary party she was going to. Charlie explained that she had hoped to be a secretary in a law firm but never seemed to get enough money together to go to business school, seeing as how she spent so much money on her clothes and accessories.

She had never married, but she'd had "close relationships" with some of her coworkers over the years, she casually confided as she pointed out a couple of the bare-chested gentlemen overhead. She didn't think she would ever find a man who would tolerate her "parties" and the cost of the wardrobe necessary for them.

Charlie's sentences were frequently suspended in air while she blew a large bubble and sucked it back in, looking satisfied if the proportions of the gum ballooned over her nose. Charlie told me, along with just about everybody else in the factory, that she had been raised in several foster homes after her parents were killed when she was six. As the story goes, her parents worked for a brewery somewhere "back East," and one day they both fell into a huge vat of hops or something and had suffocated. Their bodies weren't found for two days. Charlene told us that after she found out, years later, how her folks had met their end, she could never drink beer. Charlie always blew lots of bubbles during the recitation of this yarn, which varied slightly with each telling, but no one questioned her about it. Once, she introduced the tidbit that her parents were really involved in industrial espionage, that they'd been hired by a competing brewery, and that when their employer discovered what they were up to, he'd had them pushed into the vat.

Charlene often described the foster families with whom she had lived. They were all bizarre people in one way or another and, according to Charlie, "crazy about me."

Charlie never missed work, and I looked forward to seeing her each day. She was one of those happy, easy-going people who made you feel better just by being with them. She was a bright place in that dull, drab factory environment, and the lunch room lit up when she came jingling in. Charlie's coworkers, male and female, obviously adored her. The bare-chested men would go out of their way to give her a smile and a, "Hi, Charlie." Women were always vying for a seat at her table in the lunch room.

Of course, Charlie wasn't what you'd call a scintillating conversationalist, and at first, I was curious about her appeal. She would tell funny stories about her foibles without being self-deprecating. Like the time she received a notice that she was overdrawn. The bank called her landlord, since his name was on the application card. The landlord chided her about it, and she was embarrassed that he knew she was overdrawn.

"Now I know why they call them tellers," Charlie said. "They tell everybody when you're overdrawn."

Another time, she had borrowed a friend's jalopy while her car was being serviced. The brakes failed at the bottom of a hill, and she ran into a big Cadillac that was stopped at the red light. Knowing she was at fault, Charlie was terrified the other driver would get out and do her harm.

"But would you believe?" she gushed, pausing for reaction while she blew a gigantic bubble. "That sweet old man driving the Caddy came up to my window and said, 'Honey, it's a good thing I was here or you would never have stopped!'" Charlie clapped her hands in glee, causing a jangle-rama on both arms.

There was little damage to either vehicle, and neither of them got hurt. Charlie and the other driver ended up in a nearby coffee shop, exchanging war stories about other accidents they had been involved in.

Listening in on other lunch-table chatter, I discovered that Charlie knew the names and ages of her coworkers' children, their husbands' names, and other intimate facts of their family lives—whose mother-in-law lived with them, whose husbands were cheating, whose children had the mumps, measles, etc., and who was graduating or getting married. It was as though she were a member of their families.

I talked to a female coworker who had known Charlie for fifteen years. She admitted she had confided things to Charlie that she wouldn't tell her sister or her best friend. Even though Charlie had never been in this woman's home, she felt she could trust her with her secrets.

"There's something innocent and honest about her," the woman said. "I know she doesn't appear very sophisticated or smart, but sometimes she's an oracle. She has such a simple, forthright approach to problems that I tend to complicate."

I asked Marsha, a younger coworker, about Charlie. She had been at the plant for four years, and Charlie had trained her. When she started the job, Marsha had three small children and no husband. Early on, she told me, Charlie asked her direct questions about where her husband was (he had left Marsha when she became pregnant with their third child), who was taking care of the children (her mom), what did she do for fun (nothing), and did her husband support them (no). At first, Marsha was put off by Charlie's personal questions, but then Charlie began bringing clothing to work for the kids, claiming her neighbor's kids had outgrown them, but Marsha said a lot of them were brand new. Charlie also had a very "close" friend who worked in the county's child support division, and within a few weeks, Marsha's husband began making child support payments. At least once a week, Charlie would invite Marsha to dinner and/or a movie to get her out of the house for something besides work, and once in a while, Marsha's mom and the kids came along.

Several other coworkers had similar stories of Charlie. I discovered that her life amounted to much more than bleach bottles and glitzy clothes. She had touched many lives with her "innocent, direct approach," enriching them with her kindness and unselfishness. Charlene was respected and admired by her peers as few people are. She was what she was, and she was as comfortable in her skin and with her station in life as anyone I have known before or since. Perhaps the secret to Charlie's happiness came from being a true friend to everyone around her, loving them unconditionally, always giving of herself as only Charlie could.

—J. K. Fleming

Gifts of Sustenance and Sanctuary

Rare is the grandmother who doesn't love to show off her grandchildren: A framed portrait on the coffee table, depicting a toddler romping in the grass. A video clip of a little boy throwing his head back in laughter, his lilting voice like music. The mini photo album tucked into a proud grandma's purse filled with smiling, happy children at play, at the park, at a wedding. But the pictures crowding the photo albums of Dubbele Stern are of a different sort. There are no pictures of smiling babies peering out from those pages, no family portraits, no images of fathers looking down at their sons with unmasked pride. Yet, this elderly woman displays her own set of nachas with unadulterated joy.

In Dubbele's albums, if you get to thumb through them, you will find photographs of synagogues, lecterns, and prayer books. Of a Torah Scroll dedication celebration. Of people dancing and leaping in tight circles around a canopy. Of torches burning brightly, held high by little children parading before the new Torah.

Not long ago, while sitting beside Dubbe (as she is called by friends) at a circumcision, I learned the story behind those albums.

"I don't have anyone. Not a husband, not a sister, not a child, not a grandchild," she said. Then, with a twinkle in her eye and a sincere smile that never leaves her face, she added, "I have God."

Dubbe was dressed simply in old, worn, plain clothes that belie a woman known to have won the lottery.

"Tell me about yourself," I said.

She laughed, a delicate, tinkling laughter like the sound of the china dishes the waiters are carting away.

"I was born in Warsaw, Poland," she began. "*Tatte* [father] was very religious. But bread there wasn't, and we lived in a cellar. My parents came to live in Warsaw, from a small *shtetl* nearby, to look for a livelihood. I went to the Bais Yaakov School for Girls.

"In 1939, the war broke out. One day I was caught walking down the street, and then I was liberated by the ninth armored division," she says, opening and closing this harrowing chapter of her life in one breath—a subtle clue, perhaps, that explains her unwavering joyfulness.

I waited for more. Those history-packed words—war, 1939, the Warsaw Ghetto—dangled before me enticingly as I looked at the woman who carries all those memories in her heart.

"How old were you?" I gently prodded, searching for a side entrance to that pain-filled domain.

"I was a young girl, maybe twelve or thirteen. We were six children: Moshe, who learned in Baranovitch, Kalmen, Yankel, David, Rivkale, and me, Dubbela. I was hungry. I would go out to look for bread, my brother and I. We were always on the alert, scanning the countryside for signs of danger. I knew that if a Jewish child were to be discovered a kilometer away from the city, she would be shot.

"One day, as I was roaming the countryside, I saw a man moving cautiously along. He was using a walking stick to feel out his surroundings; he was obviously blind. As he came closer, I heard him muttering under his breath that he would share whatever food he receives with whoever would escort him. So I offered to accompany him, and he was happy. We went up to a little shack and he knocked on the door. When a Polish peasant woman opened the door, the blind man began to sing a Christian song.

Hearing him, the woman ushered us into her home and served us some soup.

"In this way, we spent a few weeks, wandering and begging, the blind man and I, knocking on doors, subsisting on a piece of bread, a plate of soup, and every now and then, an egg. Until, out of the blue, the blind man disappeared.

"Then, I was on my own again. When hunger overtook me, I would walk up to one of the little huts dotting the roads and beg the gentiles living there to give me something to eat, a corner to sleep."

Dubbele looked up at me, laughter in her eyes. "You could make a movie out of my story, eh?"

She continued: "Roaming the fields, I discovered an underground bunker where Jews were hiding out, and they allowed me to join them. Whenever our food supply ran out, we would sneak out again to search for food: some corn, a bit of flour, every bit was precious.

"One day, as I was making my way across a highway in search of a farmer, a group of SS men swooped down on all the passersbys and threw us into waiting trucks. I found myself in a transport sent to the Skarzysko-Kamienna slave labor camp. There I worked in a munitions factory, filling bullets with explosive powder and then loading heavy, sixteen-kilo barrels onto railway wagons. Later, I was sent to a munitions plant in Leipzig. With the help of the UNNRA, I came to Israel in 1948."

I asked about the rest of her family. Dubbe told me she never heard from them again.

"Maybe they died in Treblinka or of starvation in the ghetto, I'll never know." She becomes thoughtful. "My brother Moshe, who learned in Baranovitch, maybe he'll read this story and we'll find each other.

When Dubbele married her husband, Tuvia, in 1957, she put her holocaust experiences behind her. She wanted nothing more than to help produce a new generation of Jewish children. However, it was not destined to be. She never had children. Still, Dubbele's *joie de vivre* never waned. Always, she found ways to fill her life with joy, giving of herself and spreading happiness wherever she went.

"I had an interesting hobby," she said with that twinkle in her eye. "Every week, I would go out to buy a lottery ticket. There was one number I played with all the time—06151957, June 15, 1957, the date of my wedding.

"My husband would laugh. 'A million people buy the lottery,' he would say, 'and you'll be the winner? It's impossible. Don't burn up money; give it to charity, if you must.'"

Dubbele always assured him that one day she would, indeed, win the lottery.

"One afternoon, I was walking—no, dancing—down Allenby Street and humming a tune to myself when I met Mrs. Mund.

"'Dubbela, why are you singing?' she asked. 'What's making you so happy?'

"I told her, 'It's my day today. I'm on my way to buy a lottery ticket and I'm sure that I'll win.'

"Mrs. Mund was a good-hearted woman. She must have felt like humoring me. 'If you're going to win,' she said, 'let me join you. I'll be your partner in the lottery.'

"I said, 'Great, you're a holy woman, I can hardly stand next to you. You be the one to pull out the ticket.'

"'No,' she said. 'It's your day, you be the one.'

"So I bought a lottery ticket, placed the receipt in my pocket, thanked Mrs. Mund, and was on my way."

That week, Dubbele's wedding date turned out to be the winning numbers. She won $50,000—a small fortune in the late 1960s. Without a moment's hesitation, Dubbele hurried to Mrs. Mund and presented her with half the money. Mr. and Mrs. Mund were incredulous.

Smiling, she recalled their reaction. "'You didn't even have to tell us anything; we would never have known,' they protested. 'It's your money. You could build yourself a beautiful, five-story home!'

"'No, it belongs to both of us,'" I insisted. 'We made a partnership.'"

In addition to giving $25,000 to Mr. and Mrs. Mund, Dubbele also counted out $2,500 and handed it to the rabbi.

"'This is a tenth of the lottery winnings,' I told my rabbi. 'Give it to the charity of your choice.'"

The rest of the money Dubbele presented to her husband.

"I said to Tuvia, 'It's for you. What do I need?'"

Tuvia invested the money in a real estate, and Dubbele stopped buying lottery tickets.

Years passed. Tuvia Stern left this world. Dubbele was alone once again. And yet, the joy on her face and her zest for living never left her.

Eventually, Dubbele sold the property her husband had purchased and used those funds to build two synagogues: "One for my husband and one for me."

Today, if one ventures through the timeless arches and quaint twisting alleyways of the Meah Shearim neighborhood in Jerusalem, one comes across a small, humble structure. "Tuvia's Shteeble" reads the placard that hangs over the entrance. In Ashdod, a city not far away, stands another synagogue, "Beit Feige Dubba." Each sanctuary is a silent tribute to a woman who once searched for bread to nourish her body and now hungers for food to nourish her soul.

As for Dubbe, these days the octogenarian can be found inside a hospital cafeteria or a senior citizens home, feeding a forlorn patient, smiling to an elderly woman, spreading her sunshine, giving to others wherever she goes.

"I have no one," she says. "No one but my father in heaven."

And, of course, the albums filled with photos of the two synagogues she built, her greatest joy in life, her gift of sanctuary for generations to come.

—*Mirish Kiszner*

Jumping In

The wiper blades whooshed across the Toyota's windshield as Anna steered toward the exit. Heading east, she entered Route 60 and blended in with the causeway traffic. As she drove toward the hospital where her husband was in the intensive care unit after suffering a major heart attack, gray clouds hovered above, and sheets of rain pounded the area with an August thunderstorm. Thinking of Steve while driving there made her grip the wheel tighter. As her car climbed the span of a bridge, Anna admired the view of the choppy, royal blue bay beneath.

A semi cut into her lane directly ahead of her. Anna pedaled the brake and slowed, afraid to pass on the rain-slick asphalt. Suddenly, the Toyota's windshield wipers stopped, obscuring her vision for a moment. Frantic, she held her breath as she twisted the knob until the wipers began to work again and cleared the foggy window. All of a sudden, the truck jerked to the right, and its red rear lights flashed, signaling the driver had slammed on the brakes. The huge wheels squealed in response. The pungent odor of burning brakes and spilled diesel gushed in through the ventilator system of the Toyota. Anna choked. The semi jack-knifed and flipped over, landing on its side. For a few seconds, it skidded across the wet asphalt, causing a shrill grinding noise and flames to spark underneath the truck body before it came to a full stop.

Meanwhile, Anna yanked the steering wheel to a hard right, and the Toyota began to hydroplane. Her foot pounded on the brake—or so she thought. Panic-stricken, she'd actually stomped on the gas pedal, accelerating the motor and propelling her straight toward the bay. As the car soared over the embankment and plunged into the roiling water, Anna cried out, "Oh no! Someone please help me!" But no one in the other vehicles on the causeway could hear her desperate cries.

For a minute or so, the car dipped and floated along with the storm's current; then it began its slow descent into the bay. Water trickled in, forming a puddle under Anna's feet. She pressed the electronic door lock buttons over and over. They wouldn't budge. Neither would the electronic window buttons. Thoughts of doom enveloped her. In the background, she heard a muffled siren wail.

"I'm here! I don't want to drown! Please save me!" she screamed, hammering the glass with her fists.

Pressing her face against the window, Anna scanned the shoreline and shivered. Several people crowded the accident area. No one glanced in her direction. No one had heard her cries. Thinking of her husband in his hospital bed waiting for her visit, her heart lurched. He needed her. *Would she ever see him again?* Tears crept down her cheeks.

God, please help me. I can't die now, she prayed.

Anna swallowed hard and forced herself to calm down; she needed to think clearly. She remembered reading somewhere that you could push out the front windshield with your feet. She unfastened her seat belt and squeezed over to the passenger's side. By now, the water covered her ankles. After wiping away the tears, Anna placed her wet loafers flat against the glass, drew them back, and slammed the windshield with all her might. The window didn't budge. Gripping the seat to brace herself, she kicked again, harder, and a third time, even harder. No luck.

Anna relaxed her legs and opened her eyes. She was trapped. The realization sent a rush of adrenalin coursing through her body. The coffee she'd consumed that morning now churned in her stomach. Closing her eyes, Anna lifted her head and prayed her heart out. A frantic rapping on the window startled her.

"Hey, lady, I'm Gavin," said a husky voice.

She turned and saw a middle-aged man with a black mustache treading water next to her car. Her heart panged. Had God heard her prayers?

"I'm Anna, and I don't want to drown," she sobbed. Water now circled her knees.

"You won't, Anna. I'll get you out. Cover your face," he ordered.

His rammed his fist into the driver's window. But the glass held firm.

"What can I do? I'm here to help. Name's Bob," another male voice said. Anna lowered her hands to study the younger man splashing at the front of her car. He had a pleasant face, hazel eyes, and a shaved head.

"Help me break off this side mirror," said Gavin.

The two men clutched at the car, balancing their bodies with one hand as they battered the mirror with the other—to no avail. The mirror remained intact.

"Let me try something else," Bob said. He gave the mirror one swift kick with the heel of his foot. It snapped. "Thank you, karate lessons," he smiled.

Gavin took over and wrenched the mirror back and forth until it broke off.

"Are you alone in there?" Gavin asked.

"Yes." Anna wiped at her new tears. The tepid water now came to her waist.

"Okay, turn around and face the seat," he ordered.

He struck the driver's window with the mirror twice. The second hit cracked the window, shattering the glass into thousands of tiny pieces that covered the car's interior.

"Be careful. Brush away the glass so you can slide back over here," Gavin said.

Anna removed her scarf and used it to clear the seat. Then she heaved her drenched body over the console and into the driver's seat. The Toyota dipped from the added weight on the driver's side, plunging the car deeper into the water. Anna uttered a scream. The water was now inching up to her chin.

"Don't panic," Bob said in a calm, firm voice. "Take a deep breath and hold out your arms; we'll hoist you through the window."

As Anna's rescuers pulled and dragged her through the car window, she was completely submerged in the rushing water and the window's broken edges raked at her clothing, catching and tearing her pant leg. Two strong hands tugged her upward to the surface, where she gratefully gulped in air and held on tightly to their arms while she got her bearings.

"Thank God for sending you two angels. In today's world, many people won't get involved," Anna said, squeezing their arms tighter.

Behind her, the Toyota choked and took its last couple of gurgles before it sunk into the bay. Anna shuddered, thinking she could have still been inside. The men guided her back to the shoreline. Once there, she dropped to the damp sandy beach. A paramedic rushed over and checked Anna's vital signs. He wrapped a blanket around her shoulders and told her she'd be fine.

The rain had slowed to a fine mist, releasing the sun and its warmth from under the clouds. As Anna sat on the shore, she couldn't thank Bob and Gavin enough, and they learned more about what had happened. Rumor had it that the truck driver had broken his neck. A car in front of the semi had a front tire blow out, which caused the whole accident. Fire engines and paramedic vehicles now cluttered the causeway. The semi had spilled its contents in the accident, assorted frozen food, but nothing lethal. Traffic was backed up on both sides for several miles. Yellow police tape had been threaded around the initial scene.

Anna finally stopped shivering from the combination of shock and fear. The thud-thud of a helicopter overhead signaled its arrival. The police had cleared the causeway of all cars for the landing. The driver needed a quick transport to the nearest hospital. Anna whispered a silent prayer for him.

Gavin and Bob both offered to drive Anna to the hospital; each was heading into town anyway. Anna drove with Gavin, and Bob followed in his vehicle. She accepted. By now, her polyester pantsuit and loafers were slightly damp. Gavin offered his cell phone so she could call her husband to let him know why she was delayed and that she'd be there shortly. Then she called her brother-in-law to meet her at the hospital and drive her home.

When she arrived at the hospital she was advised that her husband had been upgraded to a semi-private room. Gavin and Bob trailed behind her as she marched down the hallway and located his new room. Once there, she hugged and kissed her husband.

"Steve, this is Gavin and Bob, the men who rescued me,"

"Thank you so much for saving my Anna," said Steve, shaking their hands.

Anna and the two men recounted the harrowing experience to Steve. After Gavin and Bob left,

Steve told his wife he had some good news. The doctor would discharge him in a few days, though he'd have to take it easy for several weeks, follow a special diet, and exercise daily. Anna grabbed his hands. Closing their eyes, the couple bowed their heads and thanked God for saving each of their lives.

A month later, they sent Bob and Gavin thank-you cards and generous gift certificates. Inside each card, Anna wrote that she and her husband would be eternally grateful for her "courageous water angels"—strangers who cared enough to get involved and jump into the choppy bay waters that fateful day. When we remember that we are, indeed, our brothers' and sisters' keepers and act accordingly—even when jumping in puts us in deep water—we help to make the world a better place.

—*Suzanne Baginskie*

Names and some personal details in the story have been changed to protect the privacy of those individuals and their families.

More Blessed to Give

Everything my four siblings and I needed to know about kindness and charity we learned from our mother. Her words of wisdom were planted like seeds in our childhood hearts: Say "please" and "thank you." Think before you speak. Share what you have. Because my mother's inspirations were not only spoken but demonstrated, they blossomed into beautiful truths that have guided me and my brothers and sisters throughout our lives.

A traditional wife dedicated to raising her children, my mother voiced her teachings early and often. Accounts of Jesus' kindness, stories of benevolent political heroes, and rules of etiquette were among her priorities of instruction. So was a familiar New Testament adage: *It is more blessed to give than it is to receive.* In our family, we first heard those words as part of the Episcopal order of worship, spoken as an invitation just before the offering. As small children sitting side by side on a wooden church pew, we interpreted the phrase as a stern directive to resist keeping our shiny quarters for the coke machine after church and to put them in the offering plate instead.

It did not take us long to understand that "giving rather than receiving" had a wider meaning for our mother. She believed that generosity was not only a spiritual directive; it was a way of life. Mother gave to God's church on Sunday and to God's people every day of the week. Not only was her wallet open, so, too, were her pantry, her oven, her closets, her car doors, her calendar, and her heart. A busy community leader, Mother shared her time and compassion with low-income families, mentally handicapped students, grief-stricken friends, nursing-home residents, and anyone else in need. My siblings and I often delivered her unexpected gifts, and we experienced firsthand the blessing of generosity as recipients' smiles widened and their eyes filled with grateful tears.

When Mother was in her mid-forties, my father, a gifted surgeon, died of cancer, leaving her to finish raising five teenagers. It seemed clear to all of us that she would need to turn her full attention to her own difficult situation. My mother had other plans. Suddenly thrust into the workforce, she always looked for mission-related job opportunities and over the years served as the social director of a retirement facility, an office manager for a doctor friend, the director of an early childhood center for low-income families, and the program director for a church-based early childhood program. In addition to her mission-focused work, Mother also taught Sunday school, provided temporary foster care for several youngsters in difficult situations, and was a hospice volunteer for terminally ill children.

As my brothers, sisters, and I moved into adulthood, we were acutely aware that Mother had set a high standard for service. We knew that, while we were expected to be good parents to our own children, it was also important to reach out to other families in need and to our community as a whole. With Mother's encouragement, we tried to follow her example by taking on wayward children, sharing our resources, and encouraging our own children to serve others.

It was with that legacy and Mother's continuing sense of service in mind that we approached her recent eightieth birthday. Retired now and on a limited budget, Mother still works as a substitute preschool teacher for a local church and a volunteer for a nearby primary school. She also sets aside one day a week to take a housebound neighbor to the grocery store. Other days she checks on a couple in a local assisted-living center.

Wanting to honor the eight amazing decades of her life, my siblings and I tried to think of what would really please her. A big party? A night on the town? A vacation? Nothing seemed quite right; Mother is not one for extravagance or expensive possessions.

With her birthday only a few months away, I decided to ask her advice.

"Mom," I said. "We really want to do something special for your birthday this year. What would please you the most?"

She was quiet for a moment; then she smiled and answered softly. "You know, I don't really need anything, and besides, I would rather give gifts than get one. Maybe we could do something for someone else on my birthday."

It was the answer I should have expected!

"Okay," I told her, shaking my head. "If that's what you really want."

If my mother wanted a mission project for a birthday present, who was I to deny her? Still, I wanted her to have some version of a birthday surprise.

I talked to my brothers and sisters and then spent the next few weeks exploring mission opportunities in the large city not far from where she lives:

homeless shelters, toy drives, prison ministries. My sister wondered if we could find something Mother could do closer to home, in her own town. While we considered our options as Mother's birthday was fast approaching, I grew frustrated that we didn't have a plan yet. That's when Mother, as she has done so many times before, provided the insight I needed. It came during one of our daily telephone calls; when I called, she was busy making pound cakes to give as holiday gifts.

"You know," she told me over the phone in between pouring batter into pans, "It's so great to be able to take cakes and pies to people as gifts, especially when I can't afford to buy expensive gifts."

That's it! I thought. *Mother is right. No matter whether you are rich or poor, it is a blessing to be able give gifts. Other people must feel the same as Mother. How many women with empty cupboards are wishing they could bake something special to give to their families and friends?*

The next day, I called the food pantry that served Mother's area. I told the director about my mother and her birthday wish. I asked if they ever needed baking items like flour and sugar.

"Yes!" she answered. "We get lots of canned hams and dried goods this time of year but not much of what people need to make special desserts."

I had a plan! I called my siblings to set everything up. They were each eager to help with my idea for a special surprise. On Mother's birthday, one of my sisters met me at Mother's house, ostensibly for a lunch out together. When we arrived, we revealed our gift.

"Mom, you said you wanted to do something for someone else on your birthday, so that's what we're giving you," I said.

"We're going to take you to buy and deliver baking items to the food bank," my sister continued. "They will share the food with women who, like you, want to give gifts from their kitchens but can't afford to buy the ingredients."

Hugging us, Mother beamed!

The next hour was the most fun the three of us have had together in years. Taking our instructions from Mother as she stood in the middle of the baking aisle at a local grocery store, my sister and I began filling carts, starting with flour, sugar, and yeast. Next, she suggested cake, cookie, and corn-bread mixes. With three carts full of bags and boxes, she moved down the aisle to baking soda and brown sugar. Then she stopped.

"Oh! How about these?" she pleaded in front of the specialty shelf. "They cost a little more, but they make a plain recipe really special."

"Sure!" we laughed.

Following Mother's lead, we piled her favorite items into our carts: chocolate chips, peanut butter bits, cinnamon, allspice, chopped almonds, raisins, pie fillings, icing, pastel-colored sprinkles. What a joy it was to shop for someone else—even people we would never meet. By the time we finished, our carts were almost too heavy to push. Loading our many bags into my sister's car in the cold December wind, we were all exuberant with delight.

On the drive to the food bank, we laughed until we cried as we shared stories about Mother's years of gift giving. I remembered eating her homemade mayhaw jelly day after day at summer camp after she'd brought a dozen Mason jars of it to the cafeteria cooks. My sister reminded us of how Mother made cakes for every one of our teachers as well as the secretary, custodian, and bus driver at the end of each school year. Mother told us how she had often taken loaves of her homemade bread to the nurses at the hospital where my dad had worked.

When we arrived at the food bank, we continued our celebration. The women who worked in the warehouse were thrilled to meet Mother and to be a part of her birthday wish. They helped us unload the dozens of bags from the trunk of my sister's car onto waiting shelves. As we toured the facility and were told about the families and organizations that would benefit from Mother's gift, it was heartwarming to feel the circle of Mother's generosity widen to include the food pantry workers and the many families who would receive the supplies.

When it was time to go, there were hugs all around and promises to stay in touch. Then, as a final celebration, we stood in a circle—the food bank staff, my sister, my amazing mother, as beautiful at eighty as she ever was, and me—singing, "Happy birthday, dear Beverly, happy birthday to you . . ." Mother, embarrassed by all the attention, smiled with the love that spills from her heart every day and repeated the words of wisdom she'd taught each of us and continues to live by: "It is always more blessed to give than it is to receive."

—Anne McCrady

This story was first published on Beliefnet.com in November 2004.

His Neighbor's Keeper

I had always known that Wisconsin's frosty clime was not for me, so when the opportunity to relocate to the Gulf Coast came my way, I jumped at it. A friend found a cute little blue rental house, just four blocks from the Gulf of Mexico, and before the month of June was out, I had moved in. Mostly. There were a few items I just couldn't fit in my car, so I promised my mom I would come back for them as soon as I could.

This thought nagged at me while I chatted with the friendly clerk at the grocery store or explored the lovely neighborhood I now called home. How I hated the thought of leaving the flower-scented air and the gracefully aged trees that lined my street. I often sat on the screened-in front porch and watched the children ride by on their bikes, the ladies walking their dogs, and the guys taking an evening jog.

I'd known Pascagoula was home the first time I visited, and each day I fell in love with it even more. I couldn't get enough of walking down to the water to watch the waves crash against the concrete breakers, a soft breeze calming the heat in my cheeks.

It didn't take long for me to find a job, and I decided to go to Wisconsin and get the rest of my things right away so I could just settle in completely, with all my things in my new home.

My landlords lived next door. A spry older couple, they had helped me unload my car when I moved in, and they always had a few minutes to stop and chat. The Cirlots seemed to work on their yard every day, and it was beautiful. They even had a greenhouse in their fenced back yard, which I hadn't seen yet but was certain it was filled with flowers and vegetables. The only vegetable in my yard was wild onion, which I smelled each time I cut the grass, but I dreamed of having flowers lining the driveway and around the bottoms of the huge oaks in the front yard. I supposed I should tell my landlords I was leaving for a few days. It would only be polite, and if Pascagoula was anything, it was neighborly. So I left on the porch light, walked over to the Cirlots to say my goodbyes, and headed north.

As I drove away, all the radio news stations went on and on about a tropical storm named Daniel that was headed toward the Gulf Coast. *Why would a tropical storm bother these people who've lived through hurricanes,* I wondered. Noting that some of the homes were over a hundred years old and were right across from the beach, I dismissed my concerns and concentrated on getting to Mom's, so I could get back to the warm salty paradise I'd made my own.

Five days later, I was met with an awful sight. When I turned onto my street, huge trees that had lain across the road had been cut off to allow the cars to pass. Limbs lined the sidewalks, and there wasn't a light to be seen. There was no power; that meant not only were there no lights, but there was no air conditioning either, and it was dark and stifling hot. *Wow, a tropical storm did all this?* I thought. *Good thing I love candles and my car is old enough to still have a lighter.*

I drove at a snail's pace to my driveway, exhausted from the sixteen-hour drive that had gotten me home and hoping my little house was still there. It was! I drove across some sticks and was soon in the carport. My headlights had shown more downed tree limbs but no damage to my little cottage, and my landlord's house looked okay, too. So I tramped into the house carrying my suitcase and quickly fell into bed.

For the first time, though, I felt completely alone. My mom was several states away, and I knew I'd hurt her by moving so far away. My friends were placing bets that I'd be back within a year, that this was just another short-lived adventure. Now, I wondered, *What was I doing here, in this hot, dark little house?* I knew only a handful of people in Pascagoula, and had left dozens of friends and family a thousand miles away. I rolled over and pushed my window open, listening for the sounds of croaking frogs to sing me to sleep. A single tear rolled down the side of my face, and I made myself focus on the beauty and kindness that had drawn me to the Gulf Coast. My family was only a call away, and many of my friends had promised to visit. *So paradise has thorns,* I mused as my eyelids drooped. *Well, at least there's a breeze.*

The sun woke me bright and early the next morning, and I ran to the porch, wanting to get a better look at the damage. The white-columned home across the street still stood, but my front yard looked strange. It was chock full of tree limbs, as if someone had piled them there. I tried to go out the front porch door, but it wouldn't open, so I slipped on my shoes and ran out the side door, past my car, and down the driveway. A one-hundred-year-old oak tree lay perfectly parallel to my house and my landlord's house. The tree top filled my yard. I followed the tree to the side of my little blue house and found another huge tree, a pine, lying alongside it. My neighbor's roof was intact; in fact, the whole house seemed untouched, but standing in the yard I was surrounded by giant trees lying on their sides.

I carefully picked my way to the back yard, where yet another ancient tree had fallen. This one had been in my yard. Its roots jutted to the sky, and it lay along the back side of my home. The top had smashed the landlords' greenhouse to the ground, and it was barely visible under the tree's canopy. I looked at their intact house and then at the cottage I rented, marveling that both had escaped damage.

As if on cue, I heard Mr. Cirlot calling my name. "Ms. Fran? Are you there?"

"I'm back here. I'll be right over."

As I rounded the corner, I saw him standing by my door holding a large bag of ice and two gallons of water.

"Hi, I'm glad those big ol' trees didn't get you," I said.

He smiled. "You're going to need these."

"Oh, are you sure? I hate to take your supplies."

Again he smiled a kind smile. "You'll probably need more than this. We have plenty. We're used to the storms. Do you have enough food?"

My landlord cared if I had enough food? Astounding. I'd had plenty of landlords, and I had never once seen this kindness in any of them. Perhaps that had something to do with why those monstrous trees had missed their homes.

"Yes, and Mom sent a bunch of treats with me, too," I smiled back, genuinely grateful for this new friend. "Sorry about your greenhouse."

"Oh, it was about time to replace it anyway. This just gets me goin' on it," he said. "My son-in-law will have those trees out of your yard as soon as possible, and they're usually pretty quick about getting the power back on. Next time, just fill your bathtub beforehand, so you'll have plenty of washin' water."

Yes, I thought, nodding my head, *a bath would be nice right now.*

Never in my life have I wanted to kiss a bald head as much as I wanted to kiss his. My neighbor's kindness to me, a near stranger, brought tears to my eyes.

"Don't worry," he assured me. "Things will be back to normal soon."

"Oh, I'm not worried. Just . . . thank you, Mr. Cirlot. You have no idea how much this means to me."

"It's only water," he said.

But to me it was much more than water. It was like having family next door. And in the restorative breeze of such benevolence, the loneliness of the night before drifted away.

—*Fran Roberts*

Bless the Beasts
and the Teenyboppers

When my daughter Alice was a teenager, I was the one who wanted to run away from home. I wished I were Rip Van Winkle so I could sleep until Alice became human again. The pain of watching my adorable little girl—my sweet, happy child—growing more and more insolent and argumentative by the hour, scornful of my concepts of proper behavior, dress, and speech, left me flailing. *Where had I gone wrong? What terrible mistakes had I made in child rearing?* She was my firstborn; I had no experience, but that was no excuse. Motherhood shouldn't need a manual. I felt like a failure at the most important role in my life, the role I had yearned for since I was small and playing with dolls.

Alice specialized in wanting to know the reason for every rule I laid down so she could explain to me in great detail why it was the stupidest thing she'd ever heard. Growing up, I'd known better than to question my mother's authority. If I or one of my siblings tried, Mom's answer was always the same—"Because I said so"—and we would jump to it. "Because I said so" didn't work with Alice. I know because I tried using it.

"That's a stupid reason," I was told as she continued with whatever she was doing.

I also tried my mother's silent *You'd better do what I say—and now!* stare that worked so effectively on my siblings and me when we were young. Alice just mimicked the look back at me.

I was at my wits' end. I'd tried being firm: I grounded her, threatened her, and took away privileges. I tried being soft: I reasoned with her, bribed her, praised any move toward a more agreeable attitude, no matter how slight. Nothing worked. Alice didn't respect curfews, skipped school if the surf was up and headed for the beach. She preferred raggedy, faded jeans to nicely pressed pants. Her language appalled me, when I could understand it at all. I wasn't up on 1970s jargon, and half her expressions sounded like gibberish to me as she hung on the phone with her friends. Friends seemed to be the only people she deemed worth talking to. Neither my husband nor I could engage her in a meaningful conversation anymore. She was disrespectful, irresponsible, arrogant, and stubborn. I saw a gloomy future for my once sweet daughter and felt powerless to stop her downward spiral.

Alice was out visiting with a high school friend one evening and, as usual, not home on time. It was a school night, and I was angry. As even more time ticked away, worry began to take over. I'd called the friend's house; she'd left some time ago. It wasn't that long a walk. *Where was she?*

At last, I heard the door open and close. I headed for the living room and the usual confrontation. What faced me instead was a genuinely worried person, and Alice was not one to worry about what I might say about missed curfews. Something was wrong. She moved to the couch and I followed.

"Oh, Mom, I hope I did the right thing," she said as we sat close, facing each other.

For a moment I thought she was going to fall into my arms like she did when she was little.

Then she sat back and continued, running her words together in one long sentence. "I was walking home from Lisa's, and just before I got to Wilkins Avenue I saw this cat in the street and it wasn't moving, and when I went to get it I saw it was all bloody but it was still breathing, and I couldn't leave it there."

She stopped, and then went on. "I carried it to your car and put it on the passenger floor mat—there's no blood on your car seat—and drove to the all-night vet's. He said he needed to be paid upfront because the cat needed a lot of care. We called the owners but they didn't answer, and I only had twenty-five dollars in my purse. The vet said he would take that as a down payment and try to reach the owners again tomorrow, but if he was unsuccessful, someone had to promise to pay the bill, and I said I would and signed a paper for him."

I said nothing and waited while she caught her breath.

"Oh, Mom, what if he can't reach them and the cat has to be there a long time to get better?"

Before I could respond, she reached her own answer. "I have money in my savings account," she said more quietly, almost as though she were talking to herself as she came up with a plan.

Then she looked up at me. "Mom, I couldn't let that poor kitty die in the street. I had to try to save it."

I nodded my head a couple of times, and we sat quietly for a few moments more before Alice got up.

"It's a school night; I'd better get to bed," she said and went to her room.

I followed on the way back to mine. As I passed her door, she said, "Night, Mom," and I said goodnight in return. But I didn't have a good night. I wondered what my daughter had gotten herself into. Why did she sign that paper? The vet would call the family in the morning and have them decide, not Alice, if he should treat their pet. I knew nothing about this twenty-four hour veterinarian clinic. Was the vet taking advantage of my daughter by having her sign to be responsible for whatever bill he ran up for the cat's care?

The veterinarian called the next afternoon to tell Alice he still had not reached anyone at the phone number on the cat's tags. When I came home she told me she had authorized the vet to continue treatment. She sounded at peace with her decision but added, "I hope it doesn't have to be there too many days. They may disconnect the intravenous line tomorrow."

Despite her attempted calm, Alice was worried. The bill was going to be a whopper. I was anxious too. What if the family had moved far away and this was one of those cats that attempts to return to its former home? Worse yet, what if the family had deliberately left the cat behind? I'd heard of families who dumped unwanted pets that way. Why didn't my daughter think things through before letting her heart dictate what to do?

A week went by. The telephone rang. When I answered it, a woman's voice asked to speak to Alice.

I said she was at school. (At least, that's where I hoped she was. It looked like a good beach day.)

"You have a wonderful daughter," the woman told me in a voice choked in tears.

She went on to explain that she and her family had just returned from their vacation and answered the urgent phone messages left by the all-night clinic. The veterinarian told her their cat was in his care and recovering. He said that if it had not been brought in when it was, he would not have been able to save its life. He told her how the cat had reached their clinic and the financial arrangement Alice had agreed to so that care could continue.

"You have no idea what that cat means to us. Cuddles has been part of our family since she was a kitten and our girls were babies. They've grown up together. The vet says we'll be able to bring her home tomorrow. The kids can't wait to hug Cuddles again." Her voice quivered. "God bless your daughter," she sobbed into the phone.

When Alice got home from school, I told her the good news. She whooped with joy and ran into her room to call her friends. I wondered if she was rejoicing at being freed from the financial obligation or because the cat had recovered. I decided it was both.

Some time later, finally off the telephone, she found me in the kitchen preparing dinner.

"I had to do it, Mom. You know that," she said.

I agreed. I knew something else as well, something far more important. I, too, wanted to whoop with joy that day, but not because of the cat's recovery or because Alice would not have to empty her savings account. It was because I'd learned my daughter was a good person. All of her adolescent acting out and testing the limits were nothing compared with what she had done for that absent family and their injured pet. I'm glad she was in school when the tearful owner phoned and I took the call. I got to see my daughter through another woman's eyes and realized I'd been standing too close to see my child as she really was. Her nerve-wracking teenage behaviors would pass, but her heart would remain steady, guiding her in the right direction, after all. I saw a happy future for my little girl.

—Marcia Rudoff

Circle of Compassion

Jackson enjoyed sitting on his Seattle street corner, watching the crowds hurry by. The middle-aged man was content. After all, he had his booze and a warm bed waiting for him at the homeless mission. But my widowed mother couldn't stand to see Jackson sitting there day after day. In fact, she mourned over his condition every time she walked by him on her way to and from work. Mom's life mission was to help people in need, but she wondered how to reach out to a homeless drunk.

My mother was well acquainted with the devastating effects of alcohol abuse. Twenty years earlier, my father had been killed by a drunk driver, leaving her alone to pay the mortgage, to provide for and raise three children. With a compassion born of her own tragedy, Mom would stop occasionally to visit with Jackson. But she realized more needed to be done. Finally, she decided to confront him.

"Jackson," she said, "you've got to get your act together! There's no future for you here. But, if you'll get cleaned up and sober, I'll give you a job at the Olympic Hotel." Pulling aside the lapel of her coat to reveal a name tag, she explained. "I'm in management. Just ask for 'Blackie.' They call me by my husband's last name."

Jackson burst out laughing. "I never heard such a funny thing as a white lady bein' called Blackie." he said, grinning and shaking his head, "Ain't no name for a woman!"

"It's a good Scottish surname!" Mom shot back. "Don't mock me, Jackson. I'm here to help. If you don't want help, I'll leave you to waste away on this corner. Just remember, if you want to work, come and find Blackie at the Olympic."

With that, Mom turned on her heel and stomped away.

"Blackie at the 'limpic, I'll sure remember that, ma'am," he called out between fits of laughter.

A few days later, Jackson ran out of money for booze. Desperate, he decided to take Mom up on her offer. First, he went to the mission to shower and find some clean clothes. Then, he wandered into the grandeur of Seattle's Olympic Hotel. As he stared in amazement at the marble pillars, plush oriental rugs, and luxurious leather chairs, the desk clerk called to him.

"Sir, may I help you?"

"Uh, yeah," he answered, clearing his throat. "I'm here to see Blackie."

He held his breath, waiting for the young woman to have him tossed out on the street. Instead, she picked up a phone to summon my mother.

"Well, Jackson," Mom said as she walked up to him, "you're a sight for sore eyes! Just look at you, all clean-shaven and dressed up. You look like you'll make a fine employee. Come and see what I've got for you."

Crossing more plush carpets, they ambled up a flight of stairs and entered the huge grand ballroom. It was like walking into a palace with ornate wood-work and enormous crystal chandeliers. Jackson's jaw dropped as he drank it all in. Mom had to nudge him so he'd take his eyes off the ceiling to look at the buzz of activity in the room. Workmen were busy rolling large, round tables into place and setting chairs around them, while several women adorned each table with crisp, white cloths. Another group of women were carefully pinning long table-skirts into fancy, ruffled pleats.

"This is where you'll work today," Mom announced, with all the steely confidence of a drill sergeant. "We have several hundred people coming in tonight for a banquet. I need everything done perfectly for my clients. Mr. Kim, here, will show you what to do."

Mom signaled to a small, Asian gentleman, who hurried over and bowed toward Jackson. Not knowing how else to respond, Jackson bowed back at Mr. Kim.

"Mr. Kim, this is Jackson," Mom said. "He's a good worker. Keep him busy."

"Yes, ma'am!" Mr. Kim answered in a sharp, military tone.

He immediately took Jackson to join the other workmen. As they crossed the room together, Mom overheard Mr. Kim saying, "Blackie gave me a job here too. She's a good boss, but you no goof around at this place or she'll throw you out!"

Jackson worked like a man in boot camp. As the day went on, he found himself enjoying the job and his fellow workers. Everyone treated him with respect because Blackie had brought him in. It felt good to be a productive participant in life rather than a mere observer. He figured he'd ask Mom for a permanent job at the hotel.

But then payday arrived, Jackson returned to his street corner and a drunken stupor.

When Mom saw him out on the street again, she barked, "Jackson, are you ever going to get your act together? You're a mess! And it's such a shame, because you're a good worker. But, if you'll get cleaned up again, I'll give you another job."

He couldn't believe she still cared. So, when Jackson ran out of money and booze, he returned to the Olympic, looking for Blackie.

The cycle of work and drunkenness repeated again and again, until Jackson was finally ready to give up drinking. He found help through an Alcoholics Anonymous group. The road to sobriety was long and hard. But, with help from his newfound "higher power," Jackson learned how to remain clean, sober, and working.

A decade later, my brother was involved in his own fierce battle with alcoholism. He desperately wanted to escape, but he lacked the power to resist drinking. In desperation, he randomly picked a Seattle-area Alcoholics Anonymous group. He had nowhere else to go. Our mother had made repeated attempts to help him, but all of her interventions had failed. Then she was transferred to Washington, D.C., too far away to be of help to her grown son. Her heart broke for him, but what more could she do? As it turned out, she'd already done what was needed.

At his first AA meeting, my brother followed the example of the others by standing up and saying, "My name is Blackie, and I'm an alcoholic."

After the meeting, a middle-aged man walked boldly up to my brother, glared into his eyes, and demanded, "You say your name is Blackie? Do you know a little lady named Blackie who worked at the 'limpic Hotel?"

"Yes, sir," my brother answered cautiously. "She's my mother."

"Well, then, you better get your act together!" the man shouted in his face. "Your mama is the finest woman on this earth. She's been good to old Jackson. You're not gonna hurt her anymore by bein' a drunk, you hear? We're gonna get you clean and sober, boy."

Then he grinned broadly and added, "Let me introduce you to my higher power."

Jackson welcomed the opportunity to help the son of the woman who had helped him.

In time, Jackson became my brother's AA sponsor, coaching him on the long and painful road to sobriety. He has remained sober for decades now.

But that's only part of the story. In Jackson, my brother found the father figure he desperately needed. And, out of gratitude, my brother became the son who looked after Jackson in his old age. When Jackson passed away from cancer, my brother was at his side, reading aloud from his "good book" and comforting his family.

This heartwarming circle of compassion came about because my mother didn't just walk by that homeless drunk on the street corner. She saw beyond the addiction to the man imprisoned by it, and she had the compassion and conviction to do something about it. In return, Jackson reached out to my brother. Not all acts of compassion circle around so neatly. Sometimes, we never know the results of our kindnesses. But, as I learned from my mother's selfless acts of charity, when we reach out to help someone in need, we inspire a world of good.

—Laura Bradford

Some names in the story have been changed to protect the privacy of those individuals and their families.

Not Interested

"No, no. Thank you, but I'm not interested." I hung up the phone, a bit annoyed with the persistence of the telemarketing representative, who had ignored my first refusal of the "offer" and my repeated insistence that I was not interested.

"I'm not interested." My thoughts suddenly turned to another time, not long ago, when I had said those same words in regard to my ministry schedule. Many concerts and seminars had occupied my time so completely that I was exhausted. I wanted to take a week off and just stay home. A phone call had been my first hint that God had other plans.

It was from the pastor of a church in Crane, Texas, calling to invite me to come and minister in his church. He wanted me to sing a concert and share my testimony the very next Sunday night. I did happen to have the date open, but I was really counting on worshipping in my church that Sunday —on the pew, not from the platform—and then spending a quiet evening in my own home.

"I'm really not interested," I had said. "It would be such a long drive, and I just got back from a week-long revival. Maybe another time?"

The pastor accepted my regrets, and we ended our conversation on a cordial note.

An hour later, I answered the phone only to hear that same pastor's voice once again. He had contacted several businessmen in the church and asked them to underwrite my plane ticket. Cheerfully and full of expectation, he offered to send me this plane ticket if I would reconsider coming to his church.

"See?" he prodded. "God wants you to come to Crane."

I was not happy. I didn't want to go anywhere. I didn't want to sing. I didn't want to share. I didn't want to minister. Hadn't he heard me say I wasn't interested? But in my heart I knew he was right. I knew it wasn't a coincidence that I was free the Sunday the church wanted me to come. I was sure the plane ticket was God's confirmation that I was to go to Crane. In fact, I had felt it in my spirit all along, but I was hoping God would let me slide by. God doesn't work that way. Never has, never will. It's not his way to let his children slide—not when there's a need to be met, not when there's a miracle just beyond the turn in the road, or in this case, a plane ride to Texas.

The crowd in the Crane church was small that Sunday night, probably less than two hundred. I sang. I shared. I prayed with a little girl at the altar.

What was the point? I asked myself on the flight back to Alabama. There was no great outpouring, no deluge of souls at the altar. It had been a meaningful but quiet service. Maybe I could have stayed home after all.

A month went by. Two months. Three.

On June fifth, as I routinely looked through my mail, I came across a letter postmarked from Crane. *Hmmm,* I mused. *Why won't those people leave me alone? I'm really not interested.*

I opened the letter and began to read:

"Dear Elaine,

When you gave your concert in Crane back in April, our twelve-year-old daughter, Sabrina, went to hear you. I'm sorry to say my husband and I didn't go. When she came back, she told me how beautiful it was and how much it meant to her.

On the night of April 27, a tornado struck just as we were trying to leave our trailer home, and it picked our car up, setting it down on her little body. She was killed instantly.

Today, I was going through her Bible and near the back of it, she had written, 'Elaine helped me find God.' I wanted to share this with you and tell you how thankful I am for fine people like you who give their testimony in song and other ways and touch the hearts of little girls like our precious daughter . . ."

I bowed my head in shame. Tears began to pour down my face, down my neck, and even to my chest, wetting my shirt. I dropped to my knees and ultimately lay on my face before the Lord, begging his forgiveness. How callous I had been! How selfish!

Reading that letter changed me forever. I was never again able to so frivolously close the door on an invitation to give of myself, no matter how tired I thought I was. Sometimes, God brings about his miracles through his people. Not interested? How could I ever have said that? I got to be a live extension of his hand, offering the answer to a child's question that none of us even knew she had. Later, the discovery of a simple commemoration of that night brought comfort to a mother who laid her child's body in a grave but found solace in the thought that she was really in the arms of God. I had said I wasn't interested. But God knew better.

—*Eloise Elaine Schneider*

A Village Built
with Ink and Dreams

When the local bus stopped in Sarbandan, Iran, a boy jumped to the dirt road, two chickens fluttering after him. A woman wrapped head to foot in a flowered cotton *chador*, only her dark eyes showing, stepped down next. Then my mother and I followed our Persian friend, Najmeh Najafi, from the bus.

I felt like I'd stepped onto a movie set, strange sights and sounds overwhelming my senses. A few men in pants and jackets so patched it was hard to tell original cloth from patch lounged against a little square building of clay stone that was the village store. Najmeh said the bulges in their cheeks were cloves of garlic they often chewed. Chickens and goats scampered along the dirt road. Up toward Mt. Damavend, the highest mountain in Iran, I could see clusters of domed clay houses in compounds of bare dirt with walls around them. But I wasn't at Universal Studios near my home in Pasadena, California. I was in a country none of my friends had ever visited, in a village where perhaps no American had set foot prior to our visit.

I hadn't wanted to leave my high school senior activities to come on this trip to Iran, but with every jolt of the bus from Tehran to Sarbandan, I'd grown more curious to see the things I'd read about in my mother's three books, *Persia Is My Heart, Reveille for A Persian Village,* and *A Wall and Three Willows* (by Helen Hinckley).

"I can't believe I'm actually here." Mother's face flushed with excitement.

I silently echoed her words.

She and Najmeh had collaborated on three books about Najmeh's social work in Sarbandan, but until now she had seen the village only in her imagination. I had read her books, but was still unprepared for such a startlingly different world from anything in my experience.

We followed Najmeh up a dirt road in the foothills of Mt. Damavend, the highest mountain in Iran, still capped with snow. I slipped my hand in the crook of Mother's arm as we passed the little houses I'd seen at a distance. Most of them seemed to be only one room, but neatly maintained. We passed fields that had been irrigated, perhaps under Najmeh's supervision, so that four-inch stalks of grain grew toward an azure sky. A chill March wind scattered blossoms from cherry and apricot trees at our feet and carried the smell of fresh-turned earth.

"It's just like I envisioned it," Mother murmured.

Women called from open doorways to invite us in for tea as they shelled apricot seeds. I could see how highly they regarded Najmeh.

"Look at the glass windows," Najmeh said when we accepted the invitation of one of the women and passed through a gate and courtyard into a two-room house. She explained that village homes usually had only openings for windows, and in winter the openings were covered with rags or paper. "I brought them here with money from the books."

My mom's books bought windows?

I remembered how Mother had done months of research and consulting with Najmeh, and then written the trilogy about Najmeh's social work in Iran. She'd given Najmeh half the royalties. I hoped the books sold well enough for every home in Sarbandan to have glass windows instead of rag coverings.

Our hostess poured us cups of tea from a steaming *samovar*, a brass urn with a spigot that sat atop a kind of sterno can used to heat the water. She had polished the samovar until it shone like gold. We sat on the only other visible possession—a carefully swept rug that covered much of the dirt floor. *Where was their furniture?* I wondered, and then realized the villagers probably had none.

We returned to the road after a brief visit, during which Najmeh talked for us all and Mother and I nodded and smiled. Two shaggy goats scampered toward us, close enough to touch.

"Step aside," Najmeh said. "The goats give the children milk."

An animal lover, I delighted in the goats being given the right of way over villagers. I'd also seen chickens cuddled in the arms of women and children. The chickens' eggs surely helped to sustain life too, and so, I presumed, the chickens were treasured pets.

This was something to write my friends about. At home, milk came in glass bottles and eggs came in cartons. American children watched cartoon billy goats cross fairy tale bridges.

"We hope to grow many crops so there is enough to eat," Najmeh explained as we walked.

The realization swept me that many of the people I saw in the village were hungry much of the time. Back home, I could simply open the refrigerator door for a filling snack.

When we came to the *jube,* a rock-strewn, snow-swollen stream that wove through Sarbandan, we saw two girls a little younger than me dressed in wide-legged trousers and gold and green tops. They drew drinking water into earthen jars as two toddlers played around their feet. One of the girls carried an infant in a sling made from cloth wrapped many times around her waist and up under her arms.

"Surely these girls aren't the mothers of the babies," Mother said softly. "They are younger than Sammie, but they look so old."

"We wrote about this. The girls in the village are twelve when they are given to boys of their parents' choice, and they start their families immediately."

"Yes, and it troubled me then. But seeing it is so much more difficult."

The girls and I threw each other furtive glances. I wondered what their thoughts were. They had never been to a movie, never been to a school dance. They'd been married since they were twelve. Where I lived, twelve-year-olds might not even be allowed to date. *What if my parents had married me off the year I would have entered junior high?* I thought.

I looked at Mother, a woman in her mid-fifties, dressed in a shapeless gray coat and sturdy, lace-up shoes. In her family life, she drove car pools and fixed dinner every night. In her writing life, she might be able to help these girls and others like them. I knew that everyday at home she carved out her own writing time from 8:00 A.M. to 12:00 noon, spent many afternoons reading papers or consulting with students, and taught three evening writing classes. I had resented her busy schedule sometimes. Now I understood the urgency of her work.

Najmeh nodded at the girls, then turned to us, her face brightening. "Many things are better since I came. Sheep are slaughtered in a field beyond the village now, not here on the banks of the jube, where their blood used to foul the water. And there are times to do laundry and wash dishes, and different times to draw drinking water."

At home I could turn on a water tap or pour cold water from a pitcher in the refrigerator if I was thirsty. We had sinks, washing machines, and dishwashers, not to mention hot water piped into our homes. I'd had no real sense of what an easy life I had and what desperate need existed elsewhere.

"We will go to the school next," Najmeh said. "Education will give the village girls more opportunities."

At the school, girls of elementary age sat three to a desk, listening attentively to their teacher. Before Najmeh came, only boys attended school. Now, the boys came in the mornings and the girls in the afternoons. My mother taught at Pasadena City College, and I'm sure she was impressed at how seriously these girls took their studies. *Would any of them be able to go on to college someday like I could the next year?* I wondered. *Would they have choices for careers?*

Farther on we came to the bathhouse, a building as large as two houses, and Najmeh led Mother and me inside. In the center of the large, rectangular room, naked women seated on the floor talked and laughed as they washed their hair or their squirming children, unembarrassed by our intrusion. I noted showers lining two walls without dividers or curtains and a dressing room without a door at one end, none in use at the moment. I tried not to stare and imagined that Mother, who dressed in her big closet at home, must be just as uncomfortable at the lack of privacy. Najmeh proudly explained how the bathhouse replaced bathing in the jube, offering both better sanitation and a social gathering place.

She introduced Mother to several women, who smiled shyly. Mother smiled back. I didn't know a word of Farsi, but I imagined Najmeh was explaining to them Mother's part in creating the bathhouse.

I could see how this gathering place was a wonderful thing for the women. Still, I was grateful that Najmeh didn't ask us to undress and join them.

We went next to a small structure erected by CARE. Najmeh pointed to a plaque on the wall that announced the building was a gift from the American people. I remembered how Mother had made sure Najmeh's reports of her social work in Iran were translated from Farsi into English and distributed to organizations that might support her work. CARE must have been one of those organizations. This building would soon hold machinery for the villagers to make their own textiles. A second, similar structure would hold looms for the women to weave Persian rugs.

"You will get the first carpet," Najmeh said, turning to Mother.

Mother's face beamed with delight. She had often spoken of wanting a Persian carpet but had chosen to spend her savings for this trip rather than a home furnishing. The carpet Najmeh spoke of would bring her both pleasure and the honor she obviously deserved.

Outside Sarbandan's mosque—a square of packed dirt enclosed by four mud-brick walls—we all washed our hands using a pitcher of water and basin kept there for ablutions, the ceremonial washing required before entrance. Reverently, we entered. Four times a day villagers gathered here to pray to Allah and thank him for his prophet Mohammed. Maybe it was sacrilegious, but I hoped they also thanked him for the improvements that had come to Sarbandan.

The sun shot the first streaks of a flaming red and orange sunset across the sky as we reached Najmeh's house. We sat around a low table for a delicious dinner of *chelo kabob*—rice and lamb. Soon, the villagers would light their kerosene lamps.

After dinner, I laid on a mat beside Najmeh. Images of child brides, glass windows, and three-sided school rooms with eager girls jostled in my head.

Decades later, every time I hear or read about tensions in the Middle East, I think of my trip to Sarbandan. I had the opportunity to see the world in a new way and to witness the difference one person can make in helping an underdeveloped country. What if everyone shared his or her assets and talents like my mother did? Imagine how our small, increasingly interconnected world could be changed.

—*Samantha Ducloux Waltz*

To Do Small Things
with Great Love

Monday morning. I was at the last ragged edge of a writing deadline, late with a car insurance payment, and expecting the temperature to hit 107 degrees. I'd have to get my head screwed on straight if I was going to write something that could nudge the world in a hopeful direction. The loftiness of the goal presented its own built-in speed bump. I couldn't get started.

Deciding it was too early for my mind to be awake, I did busy work: swept the kitchen floor, threw in a load of laundry, fed the family pets. As I topped off the indoor kitties drinking fountain—which aerates and filters the water—I had an "aha" moment: *The outdoor kitties could use something like this!*

The Porch Girlz—a not quite wild and not quite tame mama kitty and her two daughters—lived on our porch and five-ish acres. Maybe I'd be able to focus on writing later if I made sure they were squared away for the hot day ahead. Their usual water dish seemed inadequate for this kind of heat.

My plan involved a shopworn dishpan and a garden hose. I set the garden hose to *pffft* and laid it in the bottom of the dishpan. The pan filled slowly, and once the water level was above the hose nozzle, there was a gentle ripple on the water's surface. Perfect—just enough water movement. It wasn't filtered, but it wasn't sitting still. The Porch Girlz's opinion would be the true test.

They found the water in about a blink. They were happy, I was happy, and that could have been the end of the story.

But it wasn't. The little dishpan had a big day ahead, though I didn't realize it at the time.

By then, the insurance office was open, so my plan was to jet into town, hand deliver the payment, and jet home. Our greyhound, Mabel, looked optimistic. I thought about leaving her at home, but this would be a quick turnaround trip and the really wicked heat would come later in the day. Why miss a chance to make a greyhound smile? Besides, a friend works in the front office and loves to see Mabel.

My friend took my payment and showed me a picture of the insurance agent's young son. Wow! If I could stand by the Mediterranean Sea, I bet it would be the color of that little boy's eyes. I could hurry on with my day, or I could tell a proud dad something that would make his day. Yeah, I had to take the time. And I could tell from the agent's wide smile that I'd spread a little joy his way.

The drive home took us right past Mabel's favorite place in Rainier—the waterfront park. I didn't have to stop. But she was looking out the window and looking back at me, and we'd both been a little stir crazy with this heat wave. True, if I spent time in the park, I'd be that much further behind on my to-do list for the day, not to mention that writing deadline. But the park was like Disneyworld for The Mabes. I flipped on the right turn blinker.

Giddy with her good fortune, Mabel set a brisk pace as we did a loop around the park, stopping for all the usual sniffs and curiosities. In seemingly no time at all, we were nearly back to the car, just a stretch of sidewalk and a park bench away. The bench was usually empty, but not today. A woman sat there, her hair white as snow. I remembered my mom, the pain of her loss still fresh.

As we approached, the elderly woman on the bench offered a warm hello. I replied. I could've kept walking, but instead I slowed down for this softly smiling, unassuming lady. I guessed that most folks walked on past with a polite "hello." Mabel had better people skills than that, though, and I followed her lead. Almost before I slowed my pace, Mabel was right in front of this pretty woman with white curls. Within 30 seconds, Mabel's face was cradled in the woman's heavily creased hands. Mature faces light up in such an amazing way. I decided to sit down and chat for a while.

We learned our new friend was determined to walk all the way from her apartment by the senior center to the bank, despite her troublesome knee. She was working on her fitness, as am I; we had a common goal. But we both had our own day ahead, so we both rose to our feet. I offered her a ride, just in case, but this dainty lady was resolute. So like my mom.

Pulling out of the park, I figured that since the post office was just a hop and skip away, I may as well check for business mail. As I entered the post office, I noticed people bringing in boxes and boxes of envelopes from the back of a minivan. No one was there to hold the door open—except me. *It won't take long*, I thought. I held the door for them, and two more people with armloads of mail, and then another customer, just because, and over my shoulder I heard the words, "What a nice lady." I thought, *Anyone would do that*. But no one else did. So I held the door again as I left, because the people with the minivan were still packing in mail.

Back behind the wheel and ready to head home in earnest, I spotted our new friend from the park. She had made it as far as the post office in her walk, but she looked tired. I offered her a ride again. Still determined, she graciously but firmly declined my offer. I respectfully cheered her on, and as I began to pull away, she said "Thank you for stopping, Chris." No one had called me "Chris" since my mother had passed. I remembered telling the lady at the park that my name was Christy. I smiled and my heart did a little squeeze.

Back in my driveway, I saw the Porch Girlz draped in the shade here and there. They were not currently drinking from their dishpan. That did not mean, however, that it wasn't in use.

Baby Sister, the blind doe that has made our extended yard her second home, was drinking long and deep. Her cataracts have gotten so bad that the trek to the creek for water must be getting hard. The kitty dish was now Baby Sister's dish too.

Walking into my office, hoping to be whacked by inspiration, I stared at a framed Thoreau quote: "Be true to your work, your word, and your friends." But the cherished words didn't launch me into a clatter of keystrokes. My essay remained stalled.

Distraction came next in a crackle of crow voices. The adults had been working with the fledglings on flying, and the young were still hollering for food. But now they were perched on the hose and the dishpan! It looked like bath day for the black-feathered clan. The youngsters all had wet "baby bird hair" on the tops of their heads. I'd been wishing for a bird bath; I guess the wish was granted.

The kitties came back to drink, then another doe came and brought her twin fawns, following Baby Sister's lead. Well, the pan kept refilling, right?

I was thinking I'd have to disconnect my new setup to water the lawn, but when I went out to take care of that, I found the grass around the pan was nice and wet. I just moved the pan to let the overflow soak a new area. Sweet! What spilled over the edge watered the lawn or the flowers. Wherever I moved the little dishpan, it gave to the surrounding area—like rain on the desert.

Since my writing train of thought was clearly derailed and being near the computer was having little or no effect on getting me back on track, I started another load of laundry and noticed Mabel asking for a potty walk.

While we were out, we passed by the little dishpan and saw something that made me sad—three beautiful butterflies floating on the gently moving water. I felt awful. They were magnificent, like nature's art that should be beautifying the landscape.

I took Mabel back into the house and hurried back outside to fish the butterflies out of the water. There were completely limp, no signs of life. I carried them into the utility room and left them on the counter where it was warm and safe. Having had no experience with drowning butterflies, I didn't have any other ideas, except maybe they'd dry out.

As the sun dropped over the ridge, I sat in front of my computer with a blank look on my face. Suddenly, the porch erupted with scrambling cats.

I peered out into the twilight—yep, raccoons. They were so surreal, they moved across the yard like little aliens. I hadn't seen any for a long time, but then—voila!—they now had a new dishpan to wash their hands in and drink cold water from on this hot evening. (*Note to self: Clean dishpan thoroughly in morning. Who knows what raccoons will wash during the night?*)

At this rate, I would never get my essay written. I had the attention span of a gnat. Why not check on the butterflies—I mean, to them it's a matter of life and death, right?

As I stepped into the utility room, I understood all the power Dr. Frankenstein put into delivering his epic line, "It's alive!" My butterflies were alive! It looked so cool, three not quite dry butterflies taking baby steps all around the counter. I let them walk onto my open palm and then carried them out to a high, safe shrub, where they could finish waking up. Absolute magic.

Back in the house, now psychically chained to my desk, I determined to tackle the task at hand: a narrative essay about making the world a better place. I had struggled all day to begin a noteworthy piece, to write something profound. I wracked my brain, trying to think of some extraordinary contribution I'd made to the world . . . and drew a blank. Every altruistic thing I'd ever done seemed so small. Thinking of all the great philanthropists, I felt small. In comparison, my contributions to the world seemed like small potatoes, so small they seemed not to make any difference at all.

Small. Yep, that's how I felt.

Then I remembered a quote of Mother Teresa's: "We can do no great things; only small things with great love." And a goofy smile spread across my face. Suddenly, small felt okay. Better than okay. It was a calling, my own personal marching orders, straight from one of the greatest good Samaritans of all time.

Inspired, I searched the Internet for more Mother Teresa quotes, and another one jumped off the screen for me: "The hunger for love is much more difficult to remove than the hunger for bread."

And I realized there is not only a hunger for food in the world but also a hunger for kindness. I could do kindness. Lots and lots of kindness. Every which way, kindness.

Sure, I might never have the resources or opportunities to do the grand altruist deeds I dreamed of doing. But I could make a conscious and concerted effort to do essentially what I had instinctively done all day: small, random acts of kindness. Every time I slowed down today to honor someone else's need, I made somebody's world a little better.

So I've decided to take a lesson from Mother Teresa and from that worn dishpan and garden hose set on *pfft*. Maybe I will never feed millions of orphans in India, or build schools in Africa, or find a cure for breast cancer, or open a homeless shelter in my community. But every day, I can ease someone's thirst—for water, for kindness, for a little relief from whatever burden they carry. Maybe I can keep the trickle of compassion going, so that there's always some overflow for Mother Earth and for whoever or whatever creature happens by. Maybe, I can continue to aspire to loftier ways to change the world while doing these small things with great love.

—*Christy Caballero*

Contributors

Suzanne Baginskie ("Jumping In") lives on the west coast of Florida. After twenty-eight years, she recently retired from a law firm to pursue her writing career. She's been published in numerous anthologies, including *Cup of Comfort*® books, and magazines. In her spare time, she inspires other writers by teaching a creative writing course at a local college.

Laura Bradford ("Circle of Compassion") is a writer living in Washington State. She won grand prize in *A Cup of Comfort*® *for Families Touched by Alzheimer's*. Her stories also appear in *A Cup of Comfort*® *for New Mothers, A Cup of Comfort*® *Devotional for Mothers and Daughters,* and *A Cup of Comfort*® *Book of Christmas Prayer.*

Christy Caballero ("To Do Small Things with Great Love") lives off the beaten path in a magical world of wooded acreage, visiting deer, gentle butterflies, kitty whiskers, and greyhound grace. She escapes to the ocean with her husband as often as possible. With national awards in journalism and two Maxwell Awards from the Dog Writers Association of America, Christy now focuses primarily on her pet column and personal essays, several of which have been published in the *Cup of Comfort*® book series.

Trudy Chun ("An Oasis of Hope in a Harrowing World") is a writer, mother of two, and missionary living in Eastern Hungary. She and her family work with GoodSports International, a nonprofit organization that uses sports programs to reach out to underprivileged children. Previously, she served as editor of Beverly LaHaye's *Family Voice* magazine and as a contributor to Chuck Colson's *Breakpoint* magazine. She also has a story in A *Cup of Comfort*® *for Adoptive Families*.

Linda S. Clare ("Upon a Midnight Clear") is the award-winning author of *The Fence My Father Built*, a contemporary novel from Abingdon Press. She is also the coauthor of three nonfiction books and teaches novel, essay, and memoir writing at Lane Community College. She lives in Eugene, Oregon, with her husband, Brad, and their five wayward cats.

Lisa Ricard Claro ("Angels Afoot") is a freelance writer whose work has been published in the *Atlanta Journal-Constitution*, anthologies such as A *Cup for Comfort*® *for Dog Lovers*, and numerous online publications.

Sybilla A. Cook ("Generosity Knows No Stranger") is a freelance writer from Roseburg, Oregon. Best known for her guidebooks about Portland and the Battle of the Books program, she writes on many subjects. She is currently writing *Picture Book Marriage*, a biography of Caldecott-winning authors/illustrators Berta and Elmer Hader.

Sue Dallman-Carrizales ("Small Change Today, Philanthropy Tomorrow") lives in Denver, Colorado, with her husband, two Labradors, and a white cat. She was previously published in A *Cup of Comfort*® *for Dog Lovers*. Since being laid off from her job at a homeless shelter, she fancies herself a freelance writer.

Betty Johnson Dalrymple ("Quit Talkin' and Start Doin'"), an inspirational writer of devotions and stories, lives in Parker, Colorado. Her credits include *God Allows U-Turns for Women*, *Love Is a Verb*, and other anthologies. She enjoys traveling and golfing with her retired husband and their large blended family.

Michele Ivy Davis ("The Rubber Chicken Cure") recently moved to the San Diego area of California. She is a freelance writer whose stories and articles have appeared in a variety of magazines, newspapers, and anthologies, including *A Cup of Comfort® for Breast Cancer Survivors*. Her young adult novel, *Evangeline Brown and the Cadillac Motel*, has won national and international awards.

Sharon Elwell ("The Gratitude Effect") lives in Coalinga, California, where she recently retired from teaching high school English and now writes as her muse moves her. One of her essays appears in *A Cup of Comfort® for Friends*.

J. K. Fleming ("Bangles, Bubbles, and Blue-Collar Kindness") lives in Paradise, California, in the foothills of the Sierra Mountains, near Las Vegas. Her work has been mostly published in newspapers. She spends her time reading, writing, and traveling the world on freighters. On her last voyage, the ship was attacked by pirates, but that, she says, is another story.

John Forrest ("One Less to Count Up") retired after thirty-four years as an educator and began writing about the events and people that have enriched his life. His anthology of Christmas stories, *Angels, Stars and Trees: Tales of Christmas Magic*, is in its third printing, and his story "Ruthie's Run" appears in *A Cup of Comfort® for Inspiration*. He and his wife, Carol, live in Orillia, Canada, where they enjoy golf and winter travel to points south.

Beverly Golberg ("Frugality: It's Not Just about Penny-Pinching Anymore"), a resident of St. Paul, Minnesota, turned her energy to writing after retiring from paralegal work. Her writing has appeared in the literary journals *Ars Medica* and *Willard & Maple*, and in the *St. Paul Pioneer Press*. She reads her essays at the Wild Yam Cabaret in St. Paul.

Tanya Ward Goodman ("The Benevolence of Mindfulness") is the mother of two children and a freelance writer living in Los Angeles. Her work has been published in other *Cup of Comfort®* books, in *My Teacher Is My Hero*, and in *Literary Mama*. The 2008 recipient of the

Southwest Writers Workshop Storyteller Award, Tanya recently completed a memoir chronicling her experience with her father's battle with Alzheimer's disease.

Linda Hudson Hoagland ("A Lift Up—Not a Handout"), of North Tazewell, Virginia, has worked for the Tazewell County Public Schools as a purchase order clerk for twenty years. She has four published novels, and many of her award-winning short stories and essays have been published on the Internet and in literary journals.

Wm. Scott Hubbartt ("I Always Have Time for You") was born on Ewa Plantation, Territory of Hawaii. At seventeen, he enlisted in the United States Air Force, and twenty-eight years later he retired as a chief master sergeant. He currently writes, travels, and volunteers in disaster-relief operations. He and his Peruvian-born wife have three daughters and live in south Texas.

Lyndell King ("Of Worth and Grace") writes romantic comedy and suspense under the pen name Babe King. She lives in Tasmania, Australia, with her husband, two homeschooled sons, and a variety of animals, both domestic and wild, though none so wild as her boys. She also has essays in *A Cup of Comfort® for Cat Lovers* and *A Cup of Comfort® for Dog Lovers*.

Mirish Kiszner ("Gifts of Sustenance and Sanctuary") is a Jerusalem-based writer. Her weekly "Dear Libby" column receives thousands of letters from kids asking for advice on a multitude of topics. She is the author of *Extraordinary Stories about Ordinary People* and *Dear Libby: Real Kids Raising Real Issues and Libby's Sound Advice*.

Beth Levine ("The Face Beneath the Hood") is a freelance writer and humorist whose work has appeared in many national magazines, including *Reader's Digest, Woman's Day, Good Housekeeping,* and *Ladies' Home Journal*.

Sue Fagalde Lick ("No Prescription Needed") of South Beach, Oregon, is a freelance writer and musician. In addition to articles, short stories, and poems, she has published three books on Portuguese Americans and a writer's guide called *Freelancing for Newspapers*. Another of her stories appears in *A Cup of Comfort® for Families Touched by Alzheimer's*.

Mary Long ("Forgiving the Unforgivable") is a writer and radio talk show host living in her hometown of Chicago. Her passions include issues pertaining to women's spiritual growth and reclaiming their personal power. She is currently working on several projects regarding women's history and increasing the feminine voice in all facets of media.

Irene Martin ("A Legacy to Carry On") of Skamokawa, Washington, specializes in writing regional history. She received the Washington Governor's Heritage Award in 2000. Her recent books include *Sea Fire: Tales of Jesus and Fishing* and *The Flight of the Bumble Bee: 100 Years of the Columbia River Packers Association*.

Anne McCrady ("More Blessed to Give") is a poet, storyteller, and inspirational speaker whose writing appears internationally in journals, magazines, anthologies, and her own prize-winning poetry collections, *Along Greathouse Road* and *Under a Blameless Moon*. Anne lives with her husband, Mike, in Henderson, Texas.

Betsy McPhee ("The Sweetest Gift") graduated from the University of Michigan. She lives in Arizona, where she and her husband enjoy hiking and exploring the Southwest. She has been a substitute teacher and librarian. Although her four children are now grown, she still loves children's books. Her work has appeared in *Quiet Mountain Essays* and *Raising Arizona Kids*.

Christina Suzann Nelson ("Heroes on Harleys") lives with her husband and four children in Oregon's beautiful Willamette Valley. Aside from writing, she spends her time involved with school activities and homeschooling her youngest two children. This is her second story published in the *Cup of Comfort®* series.

Ava Pennington ("Stepping Out of My Comfort Zone") is a writer, speaker, and bible study teacher in Stuart, Florida. She has had numerous magazine articles published and contributed to eighteen anthologies, including *A Cup of Comfort*® *for Dog Lovers* and *A Cup of Comfort*® *for Writers*.

Jan Philpot ("Where Magic Lives") is a retired teacher and librarian. She is the author of thirteen teacher-resource books published by Incentive Publications and a novel, *Dream Painter*, by Hearts on Fire Books. Jan runs a campground in Kentucky with her husband, Ed, and enjoys most her role as Nana to nine grandchildren.

Lea Ellen Yarmill Reburn ("Guardian Angels") resides in beautiful Wasaga Beach, Ontario, Canada where she was born and raised. Married to Richard, she is a caregiver to many. She loves to write about life experiences—some typical, some not; a collection of essays on these escapades is likely.

Connie Rosser Riddle ("If We Eat Less, They Can Eat More") lives in Apex, North Carolina, with her husband, David. She is the mother of two sons, Brooks and Ross. Connie works as a middle school nurse and in her free time enjoys long walks, bike rides, and hanging out with her friends in the Triangle Writers Group. Her writing has appeared in professional journals.

Fran Roberts ("His Neighbor's Keeper") teaches language arts at Colmer Middle School in Pascagoula. She loves reading, writing, and warm Gulf breezes. She currently lives in Grand Bay, Alabama, with her husband, Darrel, and her three children, Joshua, Sarah, and Danielle.

Eleanor Roth ("Touching Souls") lives with her husband in Dartmouth, Massachusetts. Her short stories and articles have appeared in American, British, and Asian publications. Her first novel, *Rainbow Dust*, was published in 2005. A fan of the outdoors, she enjoys kayaking and delights in her extended family.

Deborah Royal ("The Coat off Her Back") lives in beautiful Bellingham, Washington, with her supportive and loving husband, Bill. She is an early childhood educator, mom, stepmom, grandma, writer, crafter, dancer, and lover of family and friends. Her work has been published in

A Cup of Comfort® for Families Touched by Alzheimer's as well as other publications.

Marcia Rudoff ("Bless the Beasts and the Teenyboppers") lives in Bainbridge Island, Washington, where she writes a local newspaper column and teaches memoir writing. A retired educator turned freelance writer, she has stories in several *Cup of Comfort®* books. Other interests include family, friends, travel, and volunteering.

Susan Sarver ("Making a Dent") lives in Chicago and writes for a university medical center. Her personal essays have appeared in various publications, including the *Christian Science Monitor, Reader's Digest, Country Living,* and *Mothering* magazines. She hopes to participate in another ophthalmology mission in 2010.

Eloise Elaine Schneider ("Beyond the Classroom" and "Not Interested"), a freelance writer and songwriter, lives in Alabama. Her work has appeared in anthologies as well as *Catholic Digest, Parenting Today's Teen, HomeLearning Canada, The Link,* and *Family Living* magazines. Eloise is the author of *52 Children's Moments* and *Taking Hearing Impairment to School.* She is also a curriculum author and the managing editor of Lesson Tutor, a lesson plan website.

Shelley Seale ("You Bought Me Sleep") is a freelance writer based out of Austin, Texas, but she vagabonds in any part of the world whenever possible. She has written for *National Geographic, Seattle Times, Austin Business Journal, Intrepid Travel,* and *Andrew Harper Traveler Magazine,* among others. Her new book, *The Weight of Silence: Invisible Children of India,* follows her journeys into the orphanages, streets, and slums of India.

Elizabeth Sharpe ("A Little Can Be a Lot") was a Peace Corps volunteer in rural Nepal for two years. She now lives in Seattle, Washington, where she writes and teaches. She received third place in the 2008 *Transitions Abroad* Travel Narrative Contest and has been published in *To Asia with Love—Japan* and *City Arts Magazine.*

Alaina Smith ("The Real Santa Claus") loves to write. Her stories have appeared in multiple volumes of the *Chocolate for Women*® and *Cup of Comfort*® book series as well as in other anthologies. Alaina works part-time as an executive assistant for a theater company and volunteers for progressive causes. She and her husband, Frank, live near Portland, Oregon.

Linda Stork ("Child by Child") lives in the country outside Eugene, Oregon, with her three dogs. Her story "Penny's Protection" is the lead story in *A Cup of Comfort*® *for Dog Lovers II*. In addition to writing narrative essays and short stories, she is working on her first novel.

Marlena Thompson ("Fixing a Faucet while Mending a Soul"), a writer and storyteller, lives in Falls Church, Virginia. She is the author of *A Rare & Deadly Issue*, a novel, and her nonfiction work has appeared in national magazines and anthologies, including *A Cup of Comfort*® *for Single Mothers*.

Grace Tierney ("All It Takes Is an Open Heart") is a writer and mother living in Ireland. She has written internationally and locally for everything from the local paper to anthologies, online media, coffee cans, and glossy magazines. She has published three books for writers, blogs on unusual words, and is currently writing her second chick-lit novel.

Cristina Trapani-Scott ("The Power of Pebbles") lives in Ypsilanti, Michigan, with her husband, Jay, and their two children, Joshua and Kiki. She works full-time as a staff writer for the *Tecumseh Herald*, and her regular columns have earned both National Newspaper Association and Michigan Press Association awards. She also recently received her master of fine arts degree from Spalding University.

Carol Tyx ("In Lila's Shoes") teaches American literature and writing at Mt. Mercy College in Cedar Rapids, Iowa. During the summer she volunteers with Christian Peacemaker Teams serving communities at risk for violence in Colombia, South America. Her work has been published in *Yankee*, *Kalliope*, *Sojourners*, and a chapbook, *The Fifty Poems*.

Ann Vitale ("A Better World for $50 or Less") lives in the Endless Mountains of northeastern Pennsylvania. She is a retired microbiologist, car dealer, and dog trainer. Her passion is writing and coaching writing in adult schools and community centers in nearby counties. Her publishing credits include educational books as well as short fiction and essays in anthologies, including *A Cup of Comfort® for the Grieving Heart* and *A Cup of Comfort® for Dog Lovers II.*

Samantha Ducloux Waltz ("A Village Built with Ink and Dreams") writes and teaches writing in Portland, Oregon. Her stories appear in numerous *Cup of Comfort®* and other anthologies as well as in *The Rambler* and the *Christian Science Monitor*. She has also written under the names Samantha Ducloux and Samellyn Wood.

Stefanie Wass ("Trash Talk") lives in Hudson, Ohio, with her husband and two daughters. A freelance writer, she has published articles and essays in the *Los Angeles Times*, *Seattle Times*, *Christian Science Monitor*, *Akron Beacon Journal*, *Akron Life and Leisure*, *Cleveland Magazine*, *A Cup of Comfort® for Mothers*, and other anthologies.

Joan Watt ("As You Are Able") lives on the family farm in Indiana, with her son and his family. She and her six-year-old granddaughter, Katie, explore the countryside frequently and document their discoveries in journals when they return home. Joan has published in *Guideposts*, *Indianapolis Monthly*, *Indianapolis Star*, and *Franklin Daily Journal* as well as in anthologies.

About the Editor

Colleen Sell has compiled and edited thirty-four anthologies in the Cup of Comfort® book series. A veteran writer and editor, she has authored, ghostwritten, or edited more than 100 books and served as editor-in-chief of two award-winning magazines. She and her husband, T. N. Trudeau, live in a turn-of-the-century farmhouse on a forty-acre pioneer homestead in the Pacific Northwest.